Your Welsh Corgi

CARDIGAN—PEMBROKE

By Dr. Robert J. Berndt

Compiled and Edited by
William W. Denlinger and R. Annabel Rathman

Cover Design by
Bruce Parker

DENLINGER'S
Box 76, Fairfax, Virginia 22030

Ch. Menfreyas Classical Jazz, an all breed Best in Show and Specialty winner owned by Tina and Rose Dameron, and his daughter T-Rose Rockin Roll Music, owned by John and Shirley Downey.

International Standard Book Number: 0-87714-052-9

Library of Congress Catalog Card Number: 77-087762

Foreword

Your Welsh Corgi is designed as a manual for the owner of the pet Welsh Corgi as well as for those who are interested in showing the Corgi in conformation and in obedience. The Cardigan and the Pembroke Standards are treated in separate chapters, but breeding kennels are grouped together, for a number of them breed both Cardigans and Pembrokes.

The advice on conditioning and grooming is based on the Author's experience as an exhibitor. Modifications of such advice must, however, be made in some instances because of varying characteristics of coat and conformation in the individual dog or line of dogs.

Although it is not possible to acknowledge individually all breeders, handlers, and judges who made suggestions for this book, the Author would like to express his gratitude to them and to all who contributed the photographs that have been used. The photographs reproduced here give a representation of Welsh Corgis from all parts of the country.

While the Welsh Corgi was not my first breed, it is a very special one. The Welsh Corgi captivates with his intelligence, his loyalty, his trust, and his love.

R. J. B.

A pack of Pera Cardigan Corgis bred and owned by Ray and Margaret Hickel in the high California desert.

The Author, Dr. Robert J. Berndt, with his Ch. Larklain's Spain of Bear Acres.

Contents

American and Canadian Ch. Cote de Neige Derek, multiple Best-in-Show winner owned by Douglas and Gladys Bundock.

Ch. Pera Smoke Screen Ap Keeche, CD, owned by Raymond and Margaret C. Hickel.

Douglas and Gladys Bundock's Ch. Bundocks Kiss Me Kate and a young fox.

The Welsh Corgi Puppy

In 1936 King George VI of England gave to his daughter, the Princess Elizabeth, a Pembroke Welsh Corgi and drew not only national but also international attention to the breed. The royal family's interest in Corgis has been consistent through the years, and Queen Elizabeth still owns Corgis today. English interest in the breed has been maintained because of this royal patronage. The enthusiasm of the English breeders has been contagious, and growing interest in both the Pembroke and the Cardigan Welsh Corgi is evident, especially in the United States, Canada, Australia, New Zealand, and South Africa.

The Welsh Corgi makes a good pet because of his great intelligence, his size, and his adaptability. Standing less than twelve inches at the withers means that he is small enough to live comfortably in the house without taking up more than his share of space. He is adaptable to changes in environment, food, and temperature and can make the necessary adjustment with a minimum of effort. He is so flexible that he gives the impression at times that he is not even aware that the change required any effort on his part. He is an "easy keep" in that he seems to adjust to any diet and to get full benefit from the food. Since he is such a good eater, his diet must be watched to prevent the possibility that he will become overweight.

Purchasing a family pet is an exciting event but not one that takes place every day. Since it is such an important happening, considerable planning should precede the actual purchase of the puppy. The family should take several trips to well-established breeding kennels and should attend at least one dog show to see examples of the two types of Corgis at various stages of development from puppy to full-grown adult.

Once these preliminary steps have been taken, and the family decides to buy a Welsh Corgi, then a reputable kennel should be selected for the purchase. If there is a local kennel club and it has a kennel referral service, the problem is simplified. However, since many areas do not have such a service available, it might be necessary to consult one of the national dog magazines. These magazines usually contain classified advertisements arranged in a geographical index which will simplify finding a kennel within easy driving distance. There are a number of breeders located across the country who are dedicated to the improvement of the breed and who will make a great effort in helping the prospective buyer find just the right puppy.

Pet-quality Welsh Corgi puppies will cost far less than show specimens, and it may be possible to find a half-grown dog for less money than a pet-quality puppy would cost. A six-month-old dog may not, however, be a good buy, for it is sometimes more difficult for the older dog to make the necessary adjustment as a family pet. A great deal will depend upon the personality of the individual dog.

In larger cities the classified section of the newspaper will have a column advertising pets for sale. This is also a valuable source of information for finding a kennel. Commercial pet shops located in shopping centers frequently have a large selection of various breeds readily available. Their prices are usually much higher than those charged by breeders, however, because of their overhead expenses and the need to realize a profit on a commercial investment. They often will sell pets on time-payments, which makes them especially attractive to a number of prospective buyers.

Most pet shop owners do not breed their own dogs and so in turn must find breeders who will supply them with their stock. By dealing directly with a breeder, therefore, one can save time, and possibly a little money.

The selection of the individual puppy may depend on a number of factors. Both female and male Welsh Corgis make good pets. Both can be housebroken by the usual methods. Males are usually less expensive because they are more numerous than females. This oversupply will keep the price of males lower. A lower price for a male, however, would not necessarily be the case for a show-quality dog.

A puppy should not be taken from his dam before he is eight weeks old. He may be weaned by the time he is six weeks of age, but the extra two weeks will give him greater stamina and more confidence when he finally does leave home. The puppy will also have additional time to adjust to a solid food diet, and the breeder will have time to have the puppies checked for worms and to have them inoculated. A breeder may occasionally have a "swimmer" puppy that is unable to stand when he is four or five weeks old.

One remedy for this condition is to have the veterinarian administer one cc of Vitamin E twice weekly. A small puppy would need only one-half cc.

When there are several puppies to choose from, one has an opportunity to see the personality of each puppy as it relates to the rest of the litter. Whether one is intrigued by the most aggressive and outgoing or develops a protective attitude toward the most shy, and retiring, a prospective buyer does get a clue to the future personality of the dog by observing puppy-play. Maturity and a new home environment can certainly modify a personality, but usually some of the original traits will remain.

While watching the puppy romp, the prospective buyer is able to verify that he does not limp or have any other obvious physical disability. The buyer should examine the puppy to make sure that his eyes are clear and that he has no sores or cuts on his body. Once this superficial physical examination has been completed, the buyer has an opportunity to make the decisions as to size, color, and overall balance. In many cases, however, a prospective buyer falls in love with a particular puppy and will decide to buy that one regardless of other factors to be considered or any predetermined requirements that he might have established. Many puppies are sold to impulsive buyers.

Before leaving on the final trip to purchase a puppy, one should make preparations for bringing him home. The easiest way to transport him is in a cardboard box that has a lid which can be used in case he gets too nervous and tries to jump out. Several layers of newspapers should be placed in the bottom of the box and covered with a layer of shredded newspaper or an old towel to help absorb any accident that might result from the puppy's first car ride.

The puppy will usually sit quietly in the box if he is talked to and if someone will pet him and calm him during the drive home. Occasionally a puppy will become excessively excited and try to climb out of the box. If a firm, calming hand is not enough to keep him confined, closing the lid and talking to him through it will at least keep him where he should be during the drive. At a later time, short drives in the car will accustom him to riding and will make trips to the veterinarian or long drives on vacation much more pleasant for both the dog and the owner.

As soon as the new puppy arrives home, he should be allowed to romp in a fenced exercise area in the yard. This will establish, from the very first moment he is in his new home, that he is to do certain things outside. Returning him to this same place frequently on a fixed schedule will start the housebreaking pattern promptly and should prove a most effective method.

Within a day or two after his arrival at his new home, the puppy should be taken to the veterinarian. He will undoubtedly have been given a temporary shot by the kennel owner from whom he was purchased, but this temporary shot will be good only for a period of a few months. A permanent inoculation can be given when the puppy is three months old. This precaution is extremely important for the health of the puppy and should never be neglected.

There are three common diseases to which dogs are susceptible—distemper, hepatitis, and leptospirosis. These are serious diseases and are frequently fatal when immunization has been neglected. Even though they are serious, there are effective inoculations against all three. A three-in-one shot can be administered by the veterinarian, followed at a later date by a booster shot. When the puppy is six months old he should also receive immunization against rabies.

On this first visit to the veterinarian, the puppy's nails should be clipped, for long nails cause discomfort to the dog when he walks. The owner should learn to clip the dog's nails himself, for they must be clipped every week. Learning to perform this simple chore can save a great deal of money for the owner over a period of time. (See page 35 for further information on nail clipping.) While at the veterinarian's, the dog should have his ears checked to see that they are free from wax, and he should also be checked to make certain that he is free from worms and other parasites.

A competent veterinarian will keep the dog in good health and assure a life of ten to twelve years for the Welsh Corgi as well as keep the owner from needless care and worry. The selection of the right veterinarian is a matter that should warrant serious consideration.

Occasionally a puppy's ears may fail to stand erect as they should. If, by the time the puppy is three months old, his ears are not up, they should be taped. The easiest method is to tape them from the inside. The basic material is a strip of one-eighth inch foam bonded to tape, which is sold in drug stores and is used to cover corns and bunions. A strip is cut one-half inch wide and the length of the ear. A piece of toothpick is inserted in the foam and the pad is fixed to the inside of the shaved ear, going from the base to the tip. Care should be exercised that the toothpick does not come in direct contact with the skin but is well covered by the padding. This pad can be left on for four or five days. If the ear is not erect by that time the treatment should be repeated, using a new pad.

When the new owner purchases a puppy, he will receive from the breeder a blue registration certificate issued by The American Kennel Club and a copy of the puppy's pedigree. The registration certificate will contain the information needed to complete the transfer of ownership from the breeder to the new owner. The paper contains such information as the names of the sire and the dam, the date of whelping, the color and sex of the puppy, and the registration number of the litter.

At the time of purchase the breeder must provide certain information on the reverse side of the registration certificate which will transfer ownership of the puppy to the purchaser. The certificate must be signed by the purchaser, who must then forward the certificate to The American Kennel Club along with the necessary fee specified on the certificate.

When filling out the information on the front side of the certificate, the new owner will have an opportunity to name the puppy. Two names are to be submitted. The first choice will be accepted unless it has already been used for another dog.

When the certificate is returned by The American Kennel Club, it should be kept in a safe place, for it represents the title of ownership of the dog. Information contained in this document will also be needed should the dog ever be entered in competition at a sanctioned show, or should the dog be used for breeding.

Evanwhit's Star Shine and Ch. Evanwhit's J. C. Super Star, Best-in-Show winning brace owned by Barbara A. Evans.

Ch. R J B Urraca, bred by the Author, Dr. Robert J. Berndt, and owned by Jan and Allison Schmidt. Judge, Marie A. Moore.

Ch. Pera Pili Pala, CD, owned by Raymond and Margaret C. Hickel.

Ch. T-Rose Mississippi Gambler, male Pembroke, owned by Cal Groff.

Cardigan Welsh Corgi

The American Kennel Club (AKC) recognizes only purebred dogs. It establishes rules for the breeding of these dogs and offers guidance to the breeders. The first step that must be taken in gaining AKC recognition for a breed is to establish a Standard—a detailed description for that particular breed which can be used as a measuring device for evaluating the dogs. The Standard is the result of the efforts of the breeders who have sought the recognition of the AKC for their breed. Over a period of years they have maintained careful breeding records of the dogs, including litter registrations and studbooks, and have assembled other information pertinent to the development of the breed, such as history and evolution, and importing and exporting.

After a probationary period in which the consistency of the breed has been demonstrated, The American Kennel Club allows the breed to be exhibited in the Miscellaneous Class at dog shows. Following a period of time during which the judges have had an opportunity to become familiar with the breed, and the exhibitors have had an opportunity to demonstrate that there is sufficient interest, the breed will be officially recognized and can be shown in regular breed and Group competition.

At the time the breed is recognized, the Standard of the breed is formally approved by the AKC. Judges and breeders use the Standard in determining the quality of the dogs. Standards are, however, difficult documents to prepare and to interpret. Size and weight descriptions present no problems, but for other sections of the Standard it is often difficult to interpret the exact meaning of the writers. As time goes on, tastes change and new breeders become dominant in the breed clubs, and the Standard for the breed may then be rewritten. Evolutionary changes of this type help to explain why pictures of breed winners of two or three decades ago appear quite different from those of dogs winning today.

The following is the official Standard for the Cardigan Welsh Corgi approved by The American Kennel Club.

13

Ch. Winsdown Black Dragon, co-owned by Glennis O. Miller and Joseph P. Kearns.

Ch. Winsdown Zephyr, CD, owned by John and Martha Behringer.

Ch. Merrilane's Sweet Crazy Daze, owned by Judy L. Mack.

Standard for the Cardigan Welsh Corgi

General Appearance—Low-set, sturdily built, with heavy bone and deep chest. Over-all silhouette long in proportion to height, culminating in low tail-set and fox-like brush. Expression alert and foxy, watchful yet friendly.

General Impression—A handsome, powerful, small dog, capable of both speed and endurance, intelligent, sturdy, but not coarse.

Head and Skull—Skull moderately wide and flat between the ears, with definite though moderate stop. *Muzzle* to measure about 3 inches in length, or in proportion to the skull as 3 to 5. Muzzle medium, i.e. neither too pointed nor too blunt but somewhat less fine than the Pembroke. *Nose*—Black. Nostrils of moderate size. Under-jaw clean-cut and strong. *Eyes*—Medium to large, and rather widely set, with distinct corners. Color dark to dark amber but clear. Blue eyes, or one dark and one blue eye, permissible in blue merles. *Mouth*—Teeth strong and regular, neither overshot nor undershot. Pincer (level) bite permissible but scissors bite preferred, e.g., the inner side of the front teeth resting closely over the front of the lower front teeth. *Ears*—Large and prominent in proportion to size of dog. Slightly rounded at the tips, moderately wide at the base, and carried erect, set well apart and well back, sloping slightly forward when erect. Flop ears a serious fault.

Neck—Muscular, well developed, especially in males, and in proportion to dog's build; fitting into strong, well-shaped shoulders.

Forequarters—Chest broad, deep, and well let down between forelegs. Forelegs short, strong, and slightly bowed around chest, and with distinct but not exaggerated crook below the carpus. Elbows close to side. A straight, terrier-like front is a fault.

Body—Long and strong, with deep brisket, well-sprung ribs with moderate tuck-up of loin. Topline level except for slight slope of spine above tail.

Hindquarters—Strong, with muscular thighs. Legs short and well boned.

Feet—Round and well padded. Hind dewclaws, if any, should be removed. Front dewclaws may be removed.

Tail—Long to moderately long, resembling a fox brush. Should be set fairly low on body line, carried low when standing or moving slowly, streaming out when at a dead run, lifted when tracking or excited, but never curled over the back. A rat tail or whip tail are faults.

Coat—Medium length but dense. Slightly harsh texture, but neither wiry nor silky. Weather-resistant. An overly short coat or a long and silky and/or curly coat are faults. Normal grooming and trimming of whiskers is permitted. Any trimming that alters the natural length of the coat is not permitted and is a serious fault. A distinctly long coat is a disqualification.

Size—Height approximately 12 inches at the highest point of the shoulder blades. Length usually between 36 and 44 inches from nose to tip of tail. In considering the height, weight, and length of a dog, over-all balance is a prime factor.

Accepted Colors—All shades of red. Sables. All shades of brindle. Black with or without tan or brindle points. Blue merle (blue and gray mixed with black; marbles) with or without tan or brindle points. The above colors usually with white flashings on chest, neck, feet, face or tail tip. No preference in above colors.

Disqualification
Any merlization other than blue. Excessive (over 50%) white.

Approved February 11, 1967
Revised January 1977

Ch. Pantyblaidd Piper, a Specialty Best-in-Show winner imported from Wales by Mrs. Michael Pym.

Ch. Robgwen Appolinaris Clem, imported by Alice Sims.

Ch. Glenjoy's Blue Charm of Sage, owned by Glennis O. Miller.

It is difficult to discuss the Cardigan without making some reference to the Pembroke. Even the framers of the Standard resorted to this technique to complete the picture of the muzzle. Since most Corgi lovers have studied both breeds, this procedure seems justified.

The Cardigan is the older of the two breeds and, as a result, is believed by many to be the more pure of the two. There is some evidence that there were Cardigan crosses into Pembroke lines a half century ago. There are, however, no references to the reverse of this process or the introduction of Pembroke blood into the Cardigan.

The Cardigan is the larger of the two breeds. He is taller, longer, and heavier. Not only is he definitely longer, but, in addition, his tail gives an added illusion of length. Since the original purpose of the two breeds was slightly different, it is understandable why there might be a physical difference between two breeds that are considered by many as cousins.

The Pembroke was used as a working dog in flat country while the Cardigan was bred to be a herding-type dog to be used in the low rocky hills of Cardiganshire. In order to scale the hills and be able to move among and over the rocks, the dog needed to be somewhat taller. His rear would require strength for springing and leaping in addition to the speed he would need to work cattle on flatter land.

The rear quarters of the Cardigan are narrower than those of the Pembroke, and the more closely placed legs give a more substantial base for springing. Should the rear feet turn either in or out, they would negate the strong action of the narrow rear. There is some concern among breeders today that rears are becoming too wide and as a result too weak.

Another problem with rears today is that a number of specimens can be seen that do not have a level top line. They slope up from shoulder to rear. This is usually a result of the hocks' being proportionately too long for the rest of the leg. Exaggerating the angulation in a show pose to bring the top line down does nothing, of course, to eliminate this hereditary fault.

The Cardigan is not to have straight front legs like the Pembroke or like those of a terrier. The heavy-boned legs must curve slightly inward toward the ankle in order to allow extra room for the broad and deep chest that the Standard calls for. Since the legs do curve slightly inward, the feet must angle slightly outward or the dog would not be able to maintain side-to-side balance either when gait-

17

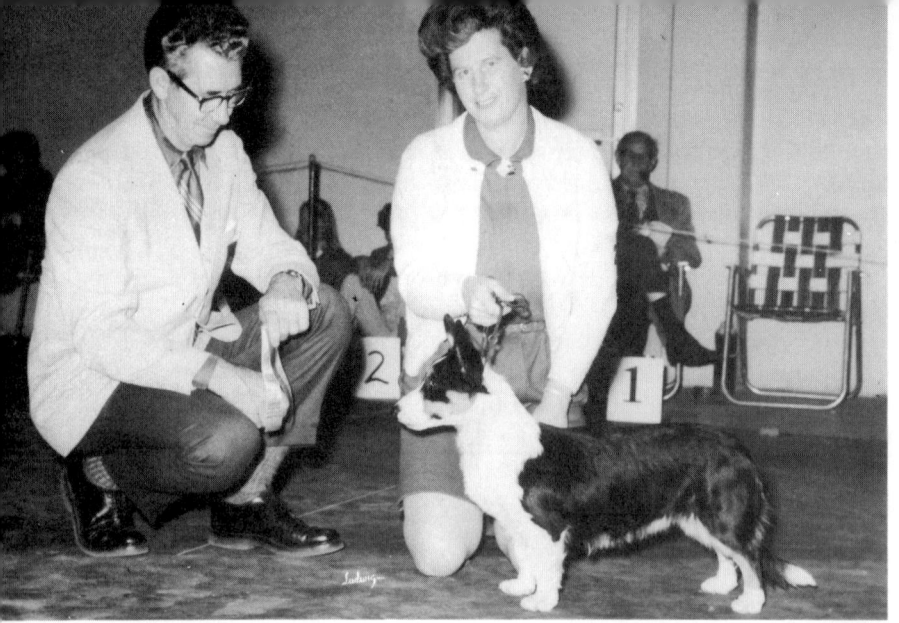

Ch. Merrilane's Sweet Foxy Lady, owned by Judy L. Mack.

ing or when standing still. If the legs were not curved the dog would move extremely wide in front and would give the impression that he was paddling. His gait would be affected greatly and would be choppy and staccato-like. The smoothness would be completely destroyed.

The tail of the Cardigan, which is to resemble the brush of a fox, is visually important in the breed, but besides its aesthetic value, it also has a physical function for a dog working in rocky terrain. The tail could serve as a sighting flag for the master trying to sight on his dog in the distance. It would also serve as an extra balancing element as the dog moves from rock to rock, much in the same way that the tail of the squirrel serves to stabilize equilibrium. The tail of the Cardigan must, therefore, be properly furnished and of correct length in proportion to the dog or its original function would be defeated. A tail that is poorly furnished would not be easy to sight nor would it carry the proper weight to serve as an extended balance.

The coat of the Cardigan is not so fine as that of the Pembroke. To protect the early specimens of the breed from the mountain dampness and the invigorating temperatures, as well as from the frequent rains, a coat of medium length and harsh texture would have been essential. A thin wiry coat or a silky one would not give the proper insulation and neither would a short coat. In the natu-

Ch. Eastwyn Miss Friendly, owned by Paul and Doris Slaboda.

ral habitat, the long coats, which are generally softer and sometimes even woolly, would be very bad, for they would retain excessive moisture and offset the insulating qualities that the correct type of coat might give. Coat length and coat texture are two of the more serious problems of the Cardigan as seen in the ring today. While the true functional value of the coat of a show dog would not need to be that of a mountain worker, this hereditary fault should be eliminated. The problem of the gay tail is also of concern and would be a defect in sighting the dog in the field. The early Pomeranian crosses may help to explain the curved tail carried up and over the back.

Color, like coat length and texture, deserves more attention than it is getting. Color concern is not serious today in reds, blacks, and tricolors, for dominant color genes have become reasonably well stabilized in these colors. Brindles and blue merles, on the other hand, are plagued by recessive color genes complicated by color dilution. Red and golden yellow traces can be seen in a number of specimens today, and diluted blue merles and golden-brindles can be seen winning in the ring. Historically, these colors may be traced to the early outcrosses with the "Red Heelers." It may also be explained by lack of attention in selective breedings on the part of the breeders.

19

American and
Canadian Ch. Pen-
broch Ufudd, Best-
in-Show winner
co-owned by
Michael Sauve and
Ruth Cooper.

Ch. Menfreyas
Classical Jazz, co-
owned by Tina
Dameron and
Rachel M. Blair.

Ch. Katydid's
Babeta, owned by
the Author.

Pembroke Welsh Corgi

To the casual observer, the Cardigan and the Pembroke Welsh Corgis may appear identical with the exception of the tail. This is really not the case. They are two distinct breeds today, and even though the language in some parts of the Standards may be similar, differences do exist. The Standard for the Pembroke Welsh Corgi is much longer than that of the Cardigan and more detailed. Many more faults are listed for the Pembroke and there is greater emphasis placed on the importance of coat color. Movement is also more clearly defined for the Pembroke than for the Cardigan.

Standard for the Pembroke Welsh Corgi

General Appearance—Low-set, strong, sturdily built and active, giving an impression of substance and stamina in a small space. Should not be so low and heavy-boned as to appear coarse or overdone, nor so light-boned as to appear racy. Outlook bold, but kindly. Expression intelligent and interested. Never shy nor vicious.

Size and Proportions—Moderately long and low. The distance from the withers to base of tail should be approximately 40 percent greater than the distance from the withers to the ground. *Height* (from ground to highest point on withers) should be 10 to 12 inches. *Weight* is in proportion to size, not exceeding 30 pounds for dogs and 28 pounds for bitches. In show condition, the preferred medium-size dog of correct bone and substance will weigh approximately 27 pounds, with bitches approximately 25 pounds. Obvious oversized specimens and diminutive toylike individuals must be very seriously penalized.

Head and Skull—Head to be foxy in shape and appearance, but not sly in expression. Skull to be fairly wide and flat between the ears. Moderate amount of stop. Very slight rounding of cheek, and not filled in below the eyes, as foreface should be nicely chiseled to give a somewhat tapered muzzle. Distance from the occiput to center of stop to be greater than the distance from stop to nose tip, the proportion being five parts of total distance for the skull and three parts for the foreface. Muzzle should be neither dish-faced nor Roman-nosed. *Nose*—Black and fully pigmented.

Eyes—Oval, medium in size, not round nor protruding, nor deep-set and piglike. Set somewhat obliquely. Variations of brown in harmony with coat color. Eye rims dark, preferably black. While dark eyes enhance the expression, true black eyes are most undesirable, as are yellow or bluish eyes.

Ch. Evanwhit's
Copper Khan, CD,
owned by Barbara
A. Evans.

Ears—Erect, firm, and of medium size, tapering slightly to a rounded point. Ears are mobile, and react sensitively to sounds. A line drawn from the nose tip through the eyes to the ear tips, and across, should form an approximate equilateral triangle. Bat ears, small catlike ears, overly large weak ears, hooded ears, ears carried too high or too low, are undesirable. Button, rose or drop ears are very serious faults.

Mouth—Scissors bite, the inner side of the upper incisors touching the outer side of the lower incisors. Level bite is acceptable. Lips should be tight, with little or no fullness, and black. Overshot or undershot bite is a very serious fault.

Neck—Fairly long, of sufficient length to provide over-all balance of the dog. Slightly arched, clean and blending well into the shoulders. A very short neck giving a stuffy appearance, and a long, thin or ewe neck, are faulty.

Body—Rib cage should be well sprung, slightly egg-shaped and moderately long. Deep chest, well let down between forelegs. Exaggerated lowness intereferes with the desired freedom of movement and should be penalized. Viewed from above, the body should taper slightly to end of the loin. Loin short. Firm level topline, neither riding up to nor falling away at the croup. A slight depression behind the shoulders caused by heavier neck coat meeting the shorter body coat is permissible. Round or flat rib cage, lack of brisket, extreme length or cobbiness, are undesirable.

Forequarters—Legs short; forearms turned slightly inward, with the distance between the wrists less than between the shoulder joints, so that the front does not appear absolutely straight. Ample bone carried right down into the feet. Pasterns firm and nearly straight when viewed from the side. Weak pasterns and knuckling over are serious faults. Shoulder blades long and well laid back along the rib cage.

22

Upper arms nearly equal in length to shoulder blades. Elbows parallel to the body, not prominent, and well set back to allow a line perpendicular to the ground to be drawn from the tip of the shoulder blade through to elbow.

Hindquarters—Ample bone, strong and flexible, moderately angulated at stifle and hock. Exaggerated angulation is as faulty as too little. Thighs should be well muscled. Hocks short, parallel, and when viewed from the side are perpendicular to the ground. Barrel hocks or cowhocks are most objectionable. Slipped or double-jointed hocks are very faulty.

Tail—Docked as short as possible without being indented. Occasionally a puppy is born with a natural dock, which if sufficiently short, is acceptable. A tail up to two inches in length is allowed, but if carried high tends to spoil the contour of the topline.

Feet—Oval, with the two center toes slightly in advance of the two outer ones. Turning neither in nor out. Pads strong and feet arched. Nails short. Dewclaws on both forelegs and hind legs usually removed. Too round, long and narrow, or splayed feet are faulty.

Movement—Free and smooth. Forelegs should reach well forward, without too much lift, in unison with the driving action of hind legs. The correct shoulder assembly and well-fitted elbows allow the long, free stride in front. Viewed from the front, legs do not move in exact parallel planes, but incline slightly inward to compensate for shortness of leg and width of chest. Hind legs should drive well under the body and move on a line with the forelegs, with hocks turning neither in nor out. Feet must travel parallel to the line of motion with no tendency to swing out, cross over, or interfere with each other. Short, choppy movement, rolling or high-stepping gait, close or overly wide coming or going, are incorrect. This is a herding dog which must have the agility, freedom of movement, and endurance to do the work for which he was developed.

Ch. Rojan Way Doctor Houston, owned by Gwen L. Platt.

Color—The outer coat is to be of self colors in red, sable, fawn, black and tan, with or without white markings. White is acceptable on legs, chest, neck (either in part as as a collar), muzzle, underpants, and as a narrow blaze on head.

Very Serious Faults—

Whitelies—Body color white with red or dark markings.

Mismarks—Self colors with any area of white on back between withers and tail, on sides between elbows and back of hindquarters, or on ears. Black with white markings and no tan present.

Bluies—Colored portions of the coat have a distinct bluish or smoky cast. This coloring is associated with extremely light or blue eyes and liver or gray eye rims, nose and lip pigment.

Coat—Medium length; short, thick, weather-resistant undercoat with a coarser, longer outer coat. Over-all length varies, with slightly thicker and longer ruff around neck, chest and on the shoulders. The body coat lies flat. Hair is slightly longer on back of forelegs and underparts, and somewhat fuller and longer on rear of hindquarters. The coat is preferably straight, but some waviness is permitted. This breed has a shedding coat, and seasonal lack of undercoat should not be too severely penalized, providing the hair is glossy, healthy, and well groomed. A wiry, tightly marcelled coat is very faulty, as is an overly short, smooth and thin coat.

Very Serious Faults—

Fluffies—A coat of extreme length with exaggerated feathering on ears, chest, legs and feet, underparts and hindquarters. Trimming such a coat does not make it more acceptable.

The Corgi should be shown in its natural condition, with no trimming permitted except to tidy the feet, and if desired, remove whiskers.

Over-all Picture—Correct type, including general balance and outline, attractiveness of head piece, intelligent outlook and correct temperament, is of primary importance. Movement is especially important, particularly as viewed from the side. A dog with smooth and free gait has to be reasonably sound and must be highly regarded. A minor fault must never take precedence over the above desired qualities.

A dog must be very seriously penalized for the following faults, regardless of whatever desirable qualities the dog may present: Whitelies, Mismarks or Bluies; Fluffies; Button, Rose or Drop Ears; Overshot or Undershot Bite; Oversize or Undersize.

The judge shall dismiss from the ring any Pembroke Welsh Corgi that is vicious or excessively shy.

Approved June 13, 1972

Ch. Bear Acres Mister Snowshoes, CD, Best-in-Show winner owned by Mrs. Frank Hayward.

The Standard establishes a description of the ideal dog. While every breeder tries to produce just such an animal, it is probably safe to say that no dog with all these qualities just in the right proportion ever existed. The fact that such a dog is not a reality should in no way deter a breeder from trying to produce the ideal dog, nor a prospective owner from trying to purchase such a specimen. There are, however, some qualities that are more important than others, and special attention should be given to them when considering the breed, trying always to obtain the specimen which most closely meets the Standard.

One of the major changes that has occurred in the breed in the last few years is the increase in the weight allowance. This change in the Standard, made in 1972, increased the weight from twenty to twenty-four pounds for dogs to a maximum of thirty pounds with a preferred weight of twenty-seven. For bitches the weight was increased from eighteen to twenty-two pounds to a maximum of twenty-eight with the preferred weight being twenty-five pounds. This increase gives the dog more substance and should increase his stamina as a working dog proportionately. Since the height was not increased, it is assumed that the intention of those preparing the Standard was to give added emphasis to substance in the form of bone and muscle, which would be of great value to a true working dog that was expected to sustain himself in the field.

The head of the Pembroke Welsh Corgi is very important, for the head is what gives the necessary foxy appearance to the little dog. While the head is to have a foxy appearance, it should not have a muzzle as refined nor as snipy as that of a real fox. The muzzle of the real fox is truly narrow and pinched. The muzzle of the Pembroke should be broader in proportion to the skull than is the case with the fox. A muzzle that is too broad is equally bad, for it gives the head a coarse appearance and without the sought-for expression.

The ear set of the Pembroke is also a very important characteristic. Erect ears give the Corgi an alert and intelligent expression, just as they do the fox. The ears should be so set on the head that the tips form an equilateral triangle (i.e. all three sides of equal length) with the nose. The leg of the triangle between the ears may sometimes be shorter than the other two legs if the dog is extremely excited. However, the ears should drop back to the normal position when the dog relaxes.

The Corgi in the ring must use his ears, which are mobile and sensitive, to reflect his interest and attention. When a dog is shy,

nervous, or apprehensive in the ring, he may hold his ears back. (He will also hold them back when he is angry.) Baiting the dog in the ring almost always overcomes any tendency to hold the ears back and allows the dog to bring his ears to the correct and natural position. A Corgi with drooping ears is a most unworthy representative of the breed.

The Corgi should have a good mouth with the correct scissors bite. Being a "heeler," he was bred to control cattle by nipping at their hoofs. To be effective in this work, the teeth would have to meet properly to permit the jaws to have sufficient strength. A weak mouth resulting from a malocclusion would render the dog inadequate for the work for which he was bred.

Forequarters and hindquarters are extremely important in any working dog, for they determine the gait and the soundness of the movement. Because of the extreme shortness of leg and the width of body, the Corgi cannot have the straight terrier front that is typical of some other small dogs. When viewed from the front, the legs must taper in slightly from the perpendicular between the shoulders and the pasterns. If the legs were straight from shoulder to ankle, the dog would move wide in a paddling fashion and would lack the drive required of a working dog.

Ch. Brix's Soc-It-To-Me, owned by Bob Sims.

Greater attention seems to be given to coat quantity than in the past and longer coats are seen more frequently. Super-abundant coats are not desirable for the short-legged working dog, for they would interfere with his work in the field and the hair would become tangled with grass and tall weeds. Since many Corgis no longer work in the fields, exhibitor competition gives new emphasis to producing thicker, longer, and more lush coats. This tendency will have to be watched, for the Standard is explicit in calling for a medium coat and in penalizing extreme length.

Soundness and movement are inter-related, for movement does depend on the soundness of the dog. If the dog does not have the proper anatomical structure and the correct proportion of bone and muscle, he cannot move properly. These qualities are extremely important in all working dogs.

Ch. Wicklow's Whizzer, Best-in-Show winner owned by Mr. and Mrs. Dennis VanVelzer.

American and Canadian Ch. Cormanby Cadenza, Best-in-Show winner owned by Michael Sauve.

Conditioning the Welsh Corgi

The conditioning of the Welsh Corgi is of prime importance both for his health and for his happiness. Because the key to proper conditioning is the basic diet of the dog, a well-balanced diet should be maintained at all times. Meals can be varied to make them interesting without sacrificing standards of nutrition, and vitamin and mineral supplements can be added.

Proper nutrition is necessary for a healthy coat. To produce the correct coat, a Welsh Corgi must gain and must maintain the weight consistent with his size. Many Welsh Corgis will overeat if given the opportunity, and while the overly fat dog may be accepted as a family pet, he cannot be accepted as a show dog. Because of the ease with which a Welsh Corgi gains weight, his food must be measured. The quantity of food can be increased with increased exercise, but the dog's weight should be checked regularly to prevent unwanted gains.

In addition to a well-balanced diet, proper exercise is necessary for all dogs, so an hour or two each day should be set aside to exercise the dog. In the case of the family pet this can be accomplished by the owner's taking him for a walk or by the dog's being allowed to romp in a fenced area. A well-drained run covered with three or four inches of gravel is easy to keep clean and will keep the dog out of the mud on rainy days. An occasional lime treatment eliminates odors. Dry lime can be sprinkled over the surface and then washed through thoroughly with a hose to prevent the dog's picking it up on the pads of his feet.

Welsh Corgis need more exercise than many other breeds of dogs to stay in top shape and to maintain the correct muscle tone. When Welsh Corgis are allowed to run in groups in a large fenced area, they are able to get the necessary exercise. However, when a Welsh Corgi is alone, he will need some road work to maintain muscle tone.

Regulated exercise is important not only for the working Welsh Corgi but also for the show dog. A dog that is underexercised will not gait properly, and cannot possibly maintain the necessary balance of muscle to bone. A carefully structured training program should be established and adhered to in order to keep the Welsh Corgi in prime condition.

The Welsh Corgi that is to be exhibited should be trained in show ring pattern drills while he is still very young so that this will become a part of his routine. He should be taught the correct show pose and trained to hold the pose for the proper length of time. With this training he develops the necessary self-discipline to stand for the examination of the judge.

When the puppy is just a few weeks old he should be set up in a show pose. The feet should be placed correctly so that the puppy gets the feel of the proper position. Should the puppy move his feet, they should be re-set with a gentle but firm action. The foot is set by grasping the leg above the elbow joint, which allows the handler to control not only the motion of the foot, but of the whole leg. This assures that the dog will be in a solid, comfortable position that could not be achieved merely by twisting the foot. If the foot is not solidly placed, the dog will lean for balance, which will not be to his advantage.

A regular schedule of bathing and grooming should be established early in the puppy's life so that the owner is always well ahead of any coat problem that might arise. Brushing should start when the puppy is only a few weeks old. His coat will need very little real attention at this early age, but it will help train him for some of the longer grooming sessions which will follow at a later date. The easiest way to start training is to brush the puppy gently while holding him in your lap.

A coat must be clean to be healthy. A coat that is allowed to become dirty will tangle quickly and may develop small mats. If the coat is dirty or sticky or caked with mud, which is sometimes the case when the dog is allowed to run freely in the yard, the dog should be bathed before attempting to brush him. A partial bath or even a partial rinsing will sometimes suffice.

The Welsh Corgi changes coat with the change of seasons. In the late spring he will shed his winter undercoat prior to growing a new healthy summer coat. During this time the coat should be brushed thoroughly every day, for the old dead hair must be removed to allow the new coat to come in, and regular brushing stimulates the hair follicles and aids in new hair growth.

The Welsh Corgi requires only limited grooming to make him ready for the ring. The hair is trimmed from between the pads to increase the dog's footing as he gaits in the ring, and nails are trimmed weekly and kept as short as possible. The whiskers and the eyebrows may be trimmed even with the skin. Welsh Corgis seem to have a knack for pulling in their whiskers during trimming,

Ch. Faraway the Magic Kan-D-Kid, a multiple Best-in-Show winner co-owned by Judy Zimmerman and Robert Simpson.

but sliding the finger under the lip helps hold the whiskers out and facilitates cutting them.

The white hair of the feet and legs of the Welsh Corgi is sometimes chalked when the dog is in competition. Chalk rubbed into the white hair will serve as a dry cleaning agent and will absorb any oil or dirt that has accumulated since the dog was bathed a day or so before the show. After the chalk has been in the coat a few minutes, it should be brushed out.

The final step in readying the dog for the ring is to spray the coat with coat dressing and rub it dry with either a grooming mitt or a bristle brush.

Most Welsh Corgis are natural showmen in the ring and will need very little corrective posing. This will be especially true if the dog has been trained to pose as a puppy. He will gait easily and freely and will stop four-square if he is not caught off stride. Should he stop off-balance, the exhibitor should take an additional step, which will allow the dog to correct his pose. Another technique that may be used to correct an off-balance pose is to pull lightly on the lead so that the dog will lean away from the weight-carrying leg. This will bring him to his natural pose.

When setting the dog up on the table for the judge's examination, it may be necessary to pose each leg individually. A small table may not seem a normal place to stand, so the dog may feel uncomfortable at that height. Positioning each leg solidly gives the dog a feeling of security and allows him to be seen to his best advantage.

31

Ch. Enterprise of Brome, a Group winner who was imported by Elaine P. Erganbright.

Ch. Evanwhit's J. C. Super Star, co-owned by Barbara A. Evans and Mary Marshall.

Ch. Rozavel Field Marshal, Group winning English import co-owned by Travis Shackelford and Joan L. Maskie.

Grooming the Family Dog

Every dog should be taught from puppyhood that a grooming session is a time for business, not for play. He should be handled gently, though, for it is essential to avoid hurting him in any way. Grooming time should be pleasant for both dog and master.

A light, airy, pleasant place in which to work is desirable, and it is of the utmost importance that neither dog nor master be distracted by other dogs, cats, or people. Consequently, it is usually preferable that grooming be done indoors.

Before each session, the dog should be permitted to relieve himself. Once grooming is begun, it is important to avoid keeping the dog standing so long that he becomes tired. If a good deal of grooming is needed, it should be done in two or more short periods.

A sturdy grooming table is desirable. The dog should stand on the grooming table while the back and upper portions of his body are groomed, and lie on his side while underparts of his body are brushed, nails clipped, etc.

It is almost impossible to brush too much, and show dogs are often brushed for a full half hour a day, year round. If you cannot brush your dog every day, you should brush him a minimum of two or three times a week. Brushing removes loose skin particles and stimulates circulation, thereby improving condition of the skin. It also stimulates secretion of the natural skin oils that make the coat look healthy and beautiful.

Before brushing, any burs adhering to the coat, as well as matted hair, should be carefully removed, using the fingers and coarse toothed comb with a gentle, teasing motion to avoid tearing the coat. The coat should first be brushed lightly in the direction in which the hair grows. Next, it should be brushed in the opposite direction, a small portion at a time, making sure the bristles penetrate the hair to the skin, until the entire coat has been brushed thoroughly and all loose soil removed. Then the coat should be brushed in the direction the hair grows, until every hair is sleekly in place.

The dog that is kept well brushed needs bathing only rarely. Once or twice a year is usually enough. If it is necessary to bathe a puppy, extreme care must be exercised so that he will not become chilled. No dog should be bathed during cold weather and then permitted to go outside immediately. Whatever the weather, the dog should always be given a good run outdoors and permitted to relieve himself before he is bathed.

Various types of "dry baths" are available, and in general, they are quite satisfactory when circumstances are such that a bath in water is impractical. Dry shampoos are usually worked into the dog's coat thoroughly, then removed by towelling or brushing.

Before starting a water bath, the necessary equipment should be assembled. This includes a tub of appropriate size, preferably one that has a drain so that the water will not accumulate and the dog will not be kept standing in water throughout the bath. A rubber mat should be placed in the bottom of the tub to prevent the dog from slipping. A small hose with a spray nozzle—one that may be attached to the water faucet—is ideal for wetting and rinsing the coat, but if such equipment is not available, then a second tub or a large pail should be provided for bath and rinse water. A metal or plastic cup for dipping water, special dog shampoo, a small bottle of mineral or olive oil, and a supply of absorbent cotton should be placed nearby, as well as a supply of heavy towels, a wash cloth, and the dog's combs and brushes. Bath water and rinse water should be slightly warmer than lukewarm, but should not be hot.

To avoid accidentally getting water in the dog's ears, place a small amount of absorbent cotton in each. With the dog standing in the tub, wet his body by using the hose and spray nozzle or by using the cup to pour water over him. Take care to avoid wetting the head, and be careful to avoid getting water or shampoo in the eyes. (If you should accidentally do so, placing a few drops of mineral or olive oil in the inner corner of the eye will bring relief.) When the dog is thoroughly wet, put a small amount of shampoo on his back and work the lather into the coat with a gentle, squeezing action. Wash the entire body and then use the cup and container of water (or hose and spray nozzle) to rinse the dog thoroughly.

Dip the wash cloth into clean water, wring it out enough so it won't drip, then wash the dog's head, taking care to avoid the eyes. Remove the cotton from the dog's ears and sponge them gently, inside and out. Shampoo should never be used inside the ears, so if they are extremely soiled, sponge them clean with cotton saturated with mineral or olive oil. (Between baths, the ears should be cleaned frequently in the same way.)

Quickly wrap a towel around the dog, remove him from the tub, and towel him as dry as possible. To avoid getting an impromptu bath yourself, you must act quickly, for once he is out of the tub, the dog will instinctively shake himself.

While the hair is still slightly damp, use a clean comb or brush to remove any tangles. If the hair is allowed to dry first, it may be completely impossible to remove them.

So far as routine grooming is concerned, the dog's eyes require little attention. Some dogs have a slight accumulation of mucus in the corner of the eyes upon waking mornings. A salt solution (a teaspoon of table salt to one pint of warm, sterile water) can be sponged around the eyes to remove the stain. During grooming sessions it is well to inspect the eyes, since many breeds are prone to eye injury. Eye problems of a minor nature may be treated at home (see page 54), but it is imperative that any serious eye abnormality be called to the attention of the veterinarian immediately.

Feeding hard dog biscuits and hard bones helps to keep tooth surfaces clean. Slight discoloration may be readily removed by rubbing with a damp cloth dipped in salt or baking soda. The dog's head should be held firmly, the lips pulled apart gently, and the teeth rubbed lightly with the dampened cloth. Regular care usually keeps the teeth in good condition, but if tartar accumulates, it should be removed by a veterinarian.

If the dog doesn't keep his nails worn down through regular exercise on hard surfaces, they must be trimmed at intervals, for nails that are too long may cause the foot to spread and thus spoil the dog's gait. Neglected nails may even grow so long that they will grow into a circle and puncture the dog's skin. Nails can be cut easily with any of the various types of nail trimmers. The cut is made just outside the faintly pink bloodline that can be seen on white nails. In pigmented nails, the bloodline is not easily seen, so the cut should be made just outside the hooklike projection on the underside of the nails. A few downward strokes with a nail file will smooth the cut surface, and, once shortened, nails can be kept short by filing at regular intervals.

Care must be taken that nails are not cut too short, since blood vessels may be accidentally severed. Should you accidentally cut a nail so short that it bleeds, apply a mild antiseptic and keep the dog quiet until bleeding stops. Usually, only a few drops of blood will be lost. But once a dog's nails have been cut painfully short, he will usually object when his feet are handled.

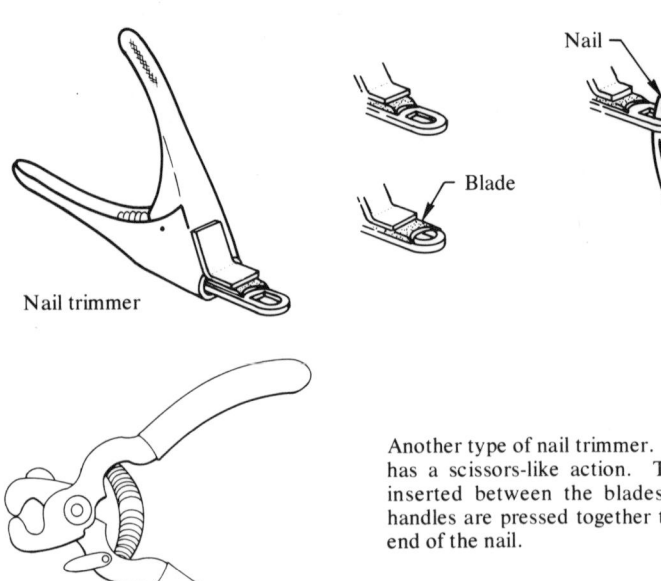

Nail

Blade

Nail trimmer

Another type of nail trimmer. This type has a scissors-like action. The nail is inserted between the blades, and the handles are pressed together to trim the end of the nail.

Dog crate with grooming-table top provides rigid, well supported surface on which to groom dog, and serves as indoor kennel for puppy or grown dog. Rubber matting provides non-slip surface. Dog's collar may be attached to adjustable arm.

Centered below is a grooming table with an adjustable arm to which the dog's collar may be attached. The adjustable arm at right below may be clamped to an ordinary table or other rigid surface which will serve as a grooming table.

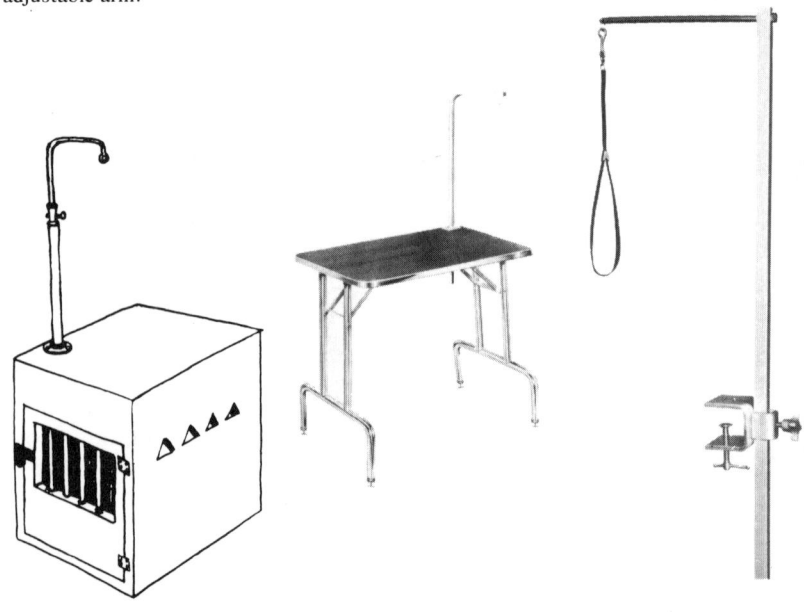

"Bed and Board" for the Family Dog

It is much easier to adapt to the demands of a new puppy if you collect the necessary equipment before you bring him home. You will need a water and food dish—preferably stainless steel and of a type that will not tip easily. You will need some chew toys, a soft puppy lead, and a soft hair brush for puppy grooming. You will need to decide where your dog is going to sleep and to prepare his bed.

Every dog should have a bed of his own, snug and warm, where he can retire undisturbed when he wishes to nap. And, especially with a small puppy, it is desirable to have the bed arranged so the dog can be securely confined at times, safe and contented. If the puppy is taught early in life to stay quietly in his box at night, or when the family is out, the habit will carry over into adulthood and will benefit both dog and master.

The dog should never be banished to a damp, cold basement, but should be quartered in an out-of-the-way corner close to the center of family activity. His bed can be an elaborate cushioned affair with electric warming pad, or simply a rectangular wooden box or heavy paper carton, cushioned with a clean cotton rug or towel. Actually, the latter is ideal for a new puppy, for it is snug, easy to clean, and expendable. A "door" can be cut on one side of the box for easy access, but it should be placed in such a way that the dog can still be confined when desirable.

The shipping crates used by professional handlers at dog shows make ideal indoor quarters. They are lightweight but strong, provide adequate air circulation, yet are snug and warm and easily cleaned. For the dog owner who takes his dog along when he travels, a dog crate is ideal, for the dog will willingly stay in his accustomed bed during long automobile trips, and the crate can be taken inside motels or hotels at night, making the dog a far more acceptable guest.

Dog crates are made of chromed metal or wood, and some have tops covered with a special rubber matting so they can be used as grooming tables. Anyone moderately handy with tools can construct a crate similar to the one illustrated on the opposite page.

Crates come in various sizes, to suit various breeds of dogs. For reasons of economy, the size selected for a puppy should be adequate for use when the dog is full grown. If the area seems too large when the puppy is small, a temporary cardboard partition can be installed to limit the area he occupies.

For the owner's convenience and to enhance the dog's sense of security, food and water dishes may be kept in the same general area where the crate is kept.

Nutrition

The main food elements required by dogs are proteins, fats, and carbohydrates. Vitamins A, B complex, D, and E are essential, as are ample amounts of calcium and iron. Nine other minerals are required in small amounts but are amply provided in almost any diet, so there is no need to be concerned about them.

The most important nutrient is protein and it must be provided every day of the dog's life, for it is essential for normal daily growth and replacement of body tissues burned up in daily activity. Preferred animal protein products are beef, mutton, horse meat, and boned fish. Visceral organs—heart, liver, and tripe—are good but if used in too large quantities may cause diarrhea (bones in large amounts have the same effect). Some veterinarians feel that pork is undesirable, while others consider lean pork acceptable as long as it is well cooked. Bacon drippings are often recommended for inclusion in the dog's diet, but this is a matter best discussed with your veterinarian since the salt in the bacon drippings might prove harmful to a dog that is not in good health. The "meat meal" used in some commercial foods is made from scrap meat processed at high temperatures and then dried. It is not quite so nutritious as fresh meat, but in combination with other protein products, it is an acceptable ingredient in the dog's diet.

Cooked eggs and raw egg yolk are good sources of protein, but raw egg white should never be fed since it may cause diarrhea. Cottage cheese and milk (fresh, dried, and canned) are high in protein, also. Puppies thrive on milk and it is usually included in the diet until the puppy is about three months of age, but when fed to older dogs it often causes diarrhea. Soy-bean meal, wheat germ meal, and dried brewers yeast are vegetable products high in protein and may be used to advantage in the dog's diet.

Vegetable and animal fats in moderate amounts should be used, especially if a main ingredient of the diet is dry or kibbled food. Fats should not be used excessively or the dog may become overweight. Generally, fats should be increased slightly in the winter and reduced somewhat during warm weather.

Carbohydrates are required for proper assimilation of fats. Dog biscuits, kibble, dog meal, and other dehydrated foods are good sources of carbohydrates, as are cereal products derived from rice, corn, wheat, and ground or rolled oats.

Vegetables supply additional proteins, vitamins, and minerals, and by providing bulk are of value in overcoming constipation. Raw or cooked carrots, celery, lettuce, beets, asparagus, tomatoes, and cooked spinach may be used. They should always be chopped or ground well and mixed with the other food. Various combinations may be used, but a good home-mixed ration for the mature dog consists of two parts of meat and one each of vegetables and dog meal (or cereal product).

Dicalcium phosphate and cod-liver oil are added to puppy diets to ensure inclusion of adequate amounts of calcium and Vitamins A and D. Indiscriminate use of dietary supplements is not only unjustified but may be harmful and many breeders feel that their over-use may lead to excessive growth as well as to overweight at maturity. Also, kidney damage in adult dogs has been traced to over-supplementation of the diet with calcium and Vitamin D.

Foods manufactured by well-known and reputable food processors are nutritionally sound and are offered in sufficient variety of flavors, textures, and consistencies that most dogs will find them tempting and satisfying. Canned foods are usually "ready to eat," while dehydrated foods in the form of kibble, meal, or biscuits may require the addition of water or milk. Dried foods containing fat sometimes become rancid, so to avoid an unpalatable change in flavor, the manufacturer may not include fat in dried food but recommend its addition at the time the water or milk is added.

Candy and other sweets are taboo, for the dog has no nutritional need for them and if he is permitted to eat them, he will usually eat less of foods he requires. Also taboo are fried foods, highly seasoned foods, and extremely starchy foods, for the dog's digestive tract is not equipped to handle them.

Frozen foods should be thawed completely and warmed at least to lukewarm, while hot foods should be cooled to lukewarm. Food should be in a fairly firm state, for sloppy food is difficult for the dog to digest.

Whether meat is raw or cooked makes little difference, so long as the dog is also given the juice that seeps from the meat during cooking. Bones provide little nourishment, although gnawing bones helps make the teeth strong and helps to keep tartar from accumulating on them. Beef bones, especially large knuckle bones, are best. Fish, poultry, and chop bones should never be given to dogs since they have a tendency to splinter and may puncture the dog's digestive tract.

Clean, fresh, cool water is essential and an adequate supply should be available twenty-four hours a day from the time the puppy is big enough to walk. Especially during hot weather, the drinking pan should be emptied and refilled at frequent intervals.

Puppies usually are weaned by the time they are six weeks old, so when you acquire a new puppy ten to twelve weeks old, he will already have been started on a feeding schedule. The breeder should supply exact details as to number of meals per day, types and amounts of food offered, etc. It is essential to adhere to this established routine, for drastic changes in diet may produce intestinal upsets. In most instances, a combination of dry meal, canned meat, and the plastic wrapped hamburger-like products provide a well-balanced diet. For a puppy that is too fat or too thin, or for one that has health problems, a veterinarian may recommend a specially formulated diet, but ordinarily, the commercially prepared foods can be used.

The amount of food offered at each meal must gradually be increased and by five months the puppy will require about twice what he needed at three months. However, the puppy should not be allowed to become too fat. Obesity has become a major health problem for dogs, and it is estimated that forty-one percent of American dogs are overweight. It is essential that weight be controlled throughout the dog's lifetime and that the dog be kept in trim condition—neither too fat nor too thin—for many physical problems can be traced directly to overweight. If the habit of overeating is developed in puppyhood, controlling the weight of the mature dog will be much more difficult.

A mature dog usually eats slightly less than he did as a growing puppy. For mature dogs, one large meal a day is usually sufficient, although some owners prefer to give two meals. As long as the dog enjoys optimum health and is neither too fat nor too thin, the number of meals a day makes little difference.

The amount of food required for mature dogs will vary. With canned dog food or home-prepared foods (that is, the combination of meat, vegetables, and meal), the approximate amount required is one-half ounce of food per pound of body weight. If the dog is fed a dehydrated commercial food, approximately one ounce of food is needed for each pound of body weight. Most manufacturers of commercial foods provide information on packages as to approximate daily needs of various breeds.

For most dogs, the amount of food provided should be increased slightly during the winter months and reduced somewhat during hot weather when the dog is less active.

As a dog becomes older and less active, he may become too fat. Or his appetite may decrease so he becomes too thin. It is necessary to adjust the diet in either case, for the dog will live longer and enjoy better health if he is maintained in trim condition. The simplest way to decrease or increase body weight is by decreasing or increasing the amount of fat in the diet. Protein content should be maintained at a high level throughout the dog's life.

If the older dog becomes reluctant to eat, it may be necessary to coax him with special food he normally relishes. Warming the food will increase its aroma and usually will help to entice the dog to eat. If he still refuses, rubbing some of the food on the dog's lips and gums may stimulate interest. It may be helpful also to offer food in smaller amounts and increase the number of meals per day. Foods that are highly nutritious and easily digested are especially desirable for older dogs. Small amounts of cooked, ground liver, cottage cheese, or mashed, hard-cooked eggs should be included in the diet often.

Before a bitch is bred, her owner should make sure that she is in optimum condition—slightly on the lean side rather than fat. The bitch in whelp is given much the same diet she was fed prior to breeding, with slight increases in amounts of meat, liver, and dairy products. Beginning about six weeks after breeding, she should be fed two meals per day rather than one, and the total daily intake increased. (Some bitches in whelp require as much as 50% more food than they consume normally.) She must not be permitted to become fat, for whelping problems are more likely to occur in overweight dogs. Cod-liver oil and dicalcium phosphate should be provided until after the puppies are weaned.

The dog used only occasionally for breeding will not require a special diet, but he should be well fed and maintained in optimum condition. A dog used frequently may require a slightly increased amount of food. But his basic diet will require no change so long as his general health is good and his flesh is firm and hard.

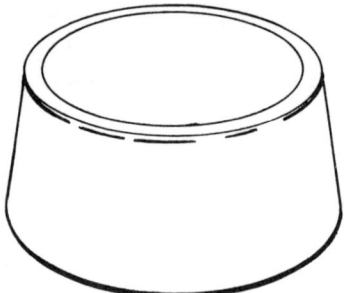

Dishes of this type are available in both plastic and stainless steel.

Crockery dish for food or water.

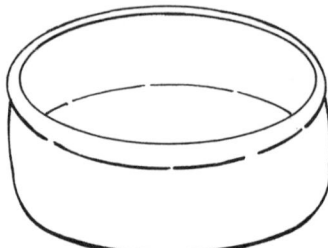

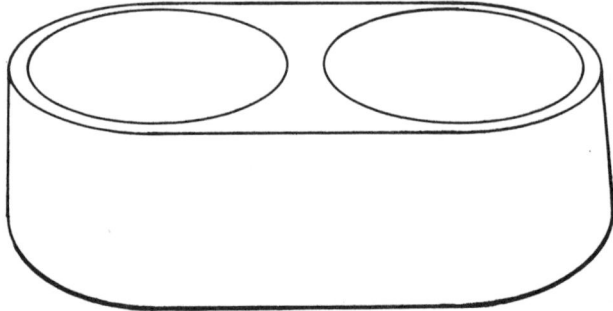

Stainless steel dish for food and water.

Maintaining the Dog's Health

In dealing with health problems, simple measures of preventive care are always preferable to cures—which may be complicated and costly. Many of the problems which afflict dogs can be avoided quite easily by instituting good dog-keeping practices in connection with feeding and housing.

Proper nutrition is essential in maintaining the dog's resistance to infectious diseases, in reducing susceptibility to organic diseases, and, of course, in preventing dietary deficiency diseases.

Cleanliness is essential in preventing the growth of disease-producing bacteria and other micro-organisms. All equipment, especially water and food dishes, must be kept immaculately clean. Cleanliness is also essential in controlling external parasites, which thrive in unsanitary surroundings.

Symptoms of Illness

Symptoms of illness may be so obvious there is no question that the dog is ill, or so subtle that the owner isn't sure whether there is a change from normal or not. **Loss of appetite, malaise** (general lack of interest in what is going on), **and vomiting** may be ignored if they occur singly and persist only for a day. However, in combination with other evidence of illness, such symptoms may be significant and the dog should be watched closely. **Abnormal bowel movements,** especially diarrhea or bloody stools, are causes for immediate concern. **Urinary abnormalities** may indicate infections, and bloody urine is always an indication of a serious condition. When a dog that has long been housebroken suddenly becomes incontinent, a veterinarian should be consulted, for he may be able to suggest treatment or medication that will be helpful.

Fever is a positive indication of illness and consistent deviation from the normal temperature range of 100 to 102 degrees is cause for concern. Have the dog in a standing position when taking his temperature. Coat the bulb of a rectal thermometer with petroleum jelly, raise the dog's tail, insert the thermometer to approximately half its length, and hold it in position for two minutes. Clean the thermometer with rubbing alcohol after each use and be sure to shake it down.

Fits, often considered a symptom of worms, may result from a variety of causes, including vitamin deficiencies, or playing to the point of exhaustion. A veterinarian should be consulted when a fit occurs, for it may be a symptom of serious illness.

Persistent coughing is often considered a symptom of worms, but may also indicate heart trouble—especially in older dogs.

Stary coat—dull and lackluster—indicates generally poor health and possible worm infestation. **Dull eyes** may result from similar conditions. Certain forms of blindness may also cause the eyes to lose the sparkle of vibrant good health.

Vomiting is another symptom often attributed to worm infestation. Dogs suffering from indigestion sometimes eat grass, apparently to induce vomiting and relieve discomfort.

Accidents and Injuries

Injuries of a serious nature—deep cuts, broken bones, severe burns, etc.—always require veterinary care. However, the dog may need first aid before being moved to a veterinary hospital.

A dog injured in any way should be approached cautiously, for reactions of a dog in pain are unpredictable and he may bite even a beloved master. A muzzle should always be applied before any attempt is made to move the dog or treat him in any way. The muzzle can be improvised from a strip of cloth, bandage, or even heavy cord, looped firmly around the dog's jaws and tied under the lower jaw. The ends should then be extended back of the neck and tied again so the loop around the jaws will stay in place.

A stretcher for moving a heavy dog can be improvised from a rug or board, and preferably two people should be available to transport it. A small dog can be carried by one person simply by grasping the loose skin at the nape of the neck with one hand and placing the other hand under the dog's hips.

Burns from chemicals should first be treated by flushing the coat with plain water, taking care to protect the dog's eyes and ears. A baking soda solution can then be applied to neutralize the chemical further. If the burned area is small, a bland ointment should be applied. If the burned area is large, more extensive treatment will be required, as well as veterinary care.

Burns from hot liquid or hot metals should be treated by applying a bland ointment, provided the burned area is small. Burns over large areas should be treated by a veterinarian.

Electric shock usually results because an owner negligently leaves an electric cord exposed where the dog can chew on it. If possible, disconnect the cord before touching the dog. Otherwise, yank the cord from the dog's mouth so you will not receive a shock when you try to help him. If the dog is unconscious, artificial respiration and stimulants will be required, so a veterinarian should be consulted at once.

Fractures require immediate professional attention. A broken bone should be immobilized while the dog is transported to the veterinarian but no attempt should be made to splint it.

Poisoning is more often accidental than deliberate, but whichever the case, symptoms and treatment are the same. If the poisoning is not discovered immediately, the dog may be found unconscious. His mouth will be slimy, he will tremble, have difficulty breathing, and possibly go into convulsions. Veterinary treatment must be secured immediately.

If you find the dog eating something you know to be poisonous, induce vomiting immediately by repeatedly forcing the dog to swallow a mixture of equal parts of hydrogen peroxide and water. Delay of even a few minutes may result in death. When the contents of the stomach have been emptied, force the dog to swallow raw egg white, which will slow absorption of the poison. Then call the veterinarian. Provide him with information as to the type of poison, and follow his advice as to further treatment.

Some chemicals are toxic even though not swallowed, so before using a product, make sure it can be used safely around pets.

Severe bleeding from a leg can be controlled by applying a tourniquet between the wound and the body, but the tourniquet must be loosened at ten-minute intervals. Severe bleeding from head or body can be controlled by placing a cloth or gauze pad over the wound, then applying firm pressure with the hand.

To treat minor cuts, first trim the hair from around the wound, then wash the area with warm soapy water and apply a mild antiseptic such as tincture of metaphen.

Shock is usually the aftermath of severe injury and requires immediate veterinary attention. The dog appears dazed, lips and tongue are pale, and breathing is shallow. The dog should be wrapped in blankets and kept warm, and if possible, kept lying down with his head lower than his body.

Bacterial and Viral Diseases

Distemper takes many and varied forms, so it is sometimes difficult for even experienced veterinarians to diagnose. It is the number one killer of dogs, and although it is not unknown in older dogs, its victims are usually puppies. While some dogs do recover, permanent damage to the brain or nervous system is often sustained. Symptoms may include lethargy, diarrhea, vomiting, reduced appetite, cough, nasal discharge, inflammation of the eyes, and a rise in temperature. If distemper is suspected, a veterinarian must be consulted at once, for early treatment is essential. Effective preventive measures lie in inoculation. Shots for temporary immunity should be given all puppies within a few weeks after whelping, and the permanent inoculations should be given as soon thereafter as possible.

Hardpad has been fairly prevalent in Great Britain for a number of years, and its incidence in the United States is increasing. Symptoms are similar to those of distemper, but as the disease progresses, the pads of the feet harden and eventually peel. Chances of recovery are not favorable unless prompt veterinary care is secured.

Infectious hepatitis in dogs affects the liver, as does the human form, but apparently is not transmissible to man. Symptoms are similar to those of distemper, and the disease rapidly reaches the acute state. Since hepatitis is often fatal, prompt veterinary treatment is essential. Effective vaccines are available and should be provided all puppies. A combination distemper-hepatitis vaccine is sometimes used.

Leptospirosis is caused by a micro-organism often transmitted by contact with rats, or by ingestion of food contaminated by rats. The disease can be transmitted to man, so anyone caring for an afflicted dog must take steps to avoid infection. Symptoms include vomiting, loss of appetite, diarrhea, fever, depression and lethargy, redness of eyes and gums, and sometimes jaundice. Since permanent kidney damage may result, veterinary treatment should be secured immediately.

Rabies is a disease that is always fatal—and it is transmissible to man. It is caused by a virus that attacks the nervous system and is present in the saliva of an infected animal. When an infected animal bites another, the virus is transmitted to the new victim. It may also enter the body through cuts and scratches that come in contact with saliva containing the virus.

All warm-blooded animals are subject to rabies and it may be transmitted by foxes, skunks, squirrels, horses, and cattle as well as dogs. Anyone bitten by a dog (or other animal) should see his physician immediately, and health and law enforcement officials should be notified. Also, if your dog is bitten by another animal, consult your veterinarian immediately.

In most areas, rabies shots are required by law. Even if not required, all dogs should be given anti-rabies vaccine, for it is an effective preventive measure.

Dietary Deficiency Diseases

Rickets afflicts puppies not provided sufficient calcium and Vitamin D. Symptoms include lameness, arching of neck and back, and a tendency of the legs to bow. Treatment consists of providing adequate amounts of dicalcium phosphate and Vitamin D and exposing the dog to sunlight. If detected and treated before reaching an advanced stage, bone damage may be lessened somewhat, although it cannot be corrected completely.

Osteomalacia, similar to rickets, may occur in adult dogs. Treatment is the same as for rickets, but here, too, prevention is preferable to cure. Permanent deformities resulting from rickets or osteomalacia will not be inherited, so once victims recover, they can be used for breeding.

External Parasites

Fleas, lice, mites, and ticks can be eradicated in the dog's quarters by regular use of one of the insecticide sprays with a four to six weeks' residual effect. Bedding, blankets, and pillows should be laundered frequently and treated with an insecticide. Treatment for external parasites varies, depending upon the parasite involved, but a number of good dips and powders are available.

Fleas may be eliminated by dusting the coat thoroughly with flea powder at frequent intervals during the summer months when fleas are a problem.

Flea collars are very effective in keeping a dog free of fleas. However, some animals are allergic to the chemicals in the collars, so caution must be observed when the collar is used and the skin of the neck area must be checked frequently and the collar removed if the skin becomes irritated. Care must also be taken that the collar is not fastened too tightly, and any excess at the end must be cut off to prevent the dog from chewing it. The collar should be removed if it becomes wet (or even damp) and should always be removed before the dog is bathed and not replaced around the dog's neck again until the coat is completely dry. For a dog which reacts to the flea collar, a medallion to be hung from the regular collar is available. This will eliminate direct skin contact and thus any allergic reaction will be avoided. The medallion should, of course, be removed when the dog is bathed.

Lice may be eradicated by applying dips formulated especially for this purpose to the dog's coat. A fine-toothed comb should

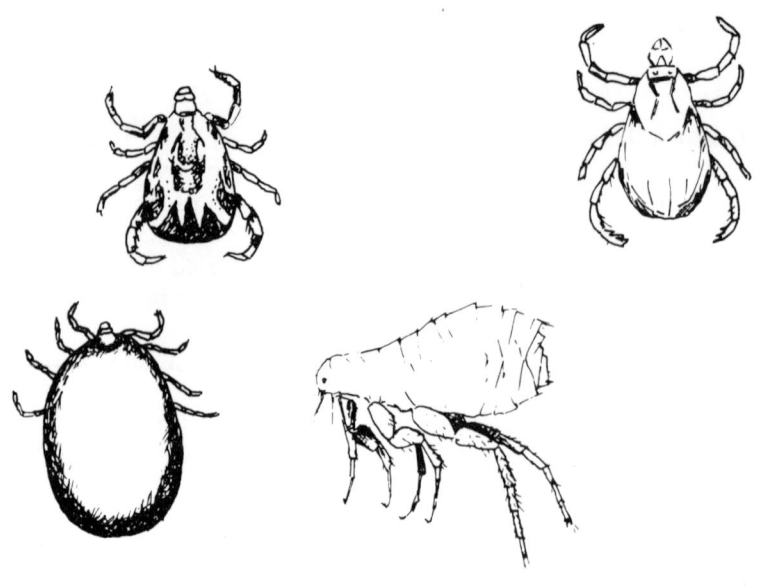

Common external parasites. Above, American dog ticks—left, female and right, male (much enlarged). Lower left, female tick, engorged. Lower right, dog flea (much enlarged).

then be used to remove dead lice and eggs, which are firmly attached to the coat.

Mites live deep in the ear canal, producing irritation to the lining of the ear and causing a brownish-black, dry type discharge. Plain mineral oil or ear ointment should be swabbed on the inner surface of the ear twice a week until mites are eliminated.

Ticks may carry Rocky Mountain spotted fever, so, to avoid possible infection, they should be removed from the dog only with tweezers and should be destroyed by burning (or by dropping them into insecticide). Heavy infestation can be controlled by sponging the coat daily with a solution containing a special tick dip.

Among other preparations available for controlling parasites on the dog's body are some that can be given internally. Since dosage must be carefully controlled, these preparations should not be used without consulting a veterinarian.

Internal Parasites

Internal parasites, with the exception of the tapeworm, may be transmitted from a mother dog to the puppies. Infestation may also result from contact with infected bedding or through access to a yard where an infected dog relieves himself. The types that may infest dogs are roundworms, whipworms, tapeworms, hookworms, and heartworms. All cause similar symptoms: a generally unthrifty appearance, stary coat, dull eyes, weakness and emaciation despite a ravenous appetite, coughing, vomiting, diarrhea, and sometimes bloody stools. Not all symptoms are present in every case, of course.

A heavy infestation with any type of worm is a serious matter and treatment must be started early and continued until the dog is free of the parasite or the dog's health will suffer seriously. Death may even result.

Promiscuous dosing for worms is dangerous and different types of worms require different treatment. So if you suspect your dog has worms, ask your veterinarian to make a microscopic examination of the feces, and to prescribe appropriate treatment if evidence of worm infestation is found.

LIFE CYCLE OF THE HEARTWORM

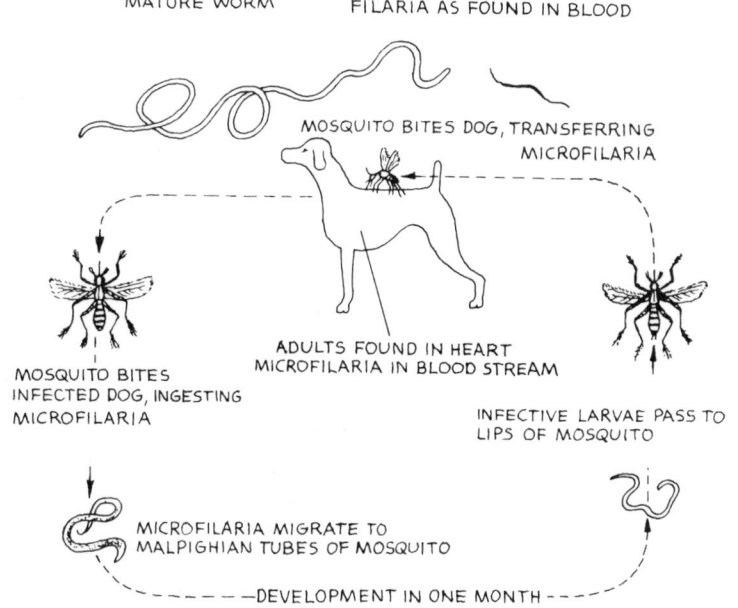

MATURE WORM

FILARIA AS FOUND IN BLOOD

MOSQUITO BITES DOG, TRANSFERRING MICROFILARIA

ADULTS FOUND IN HEART
MICROFILARIA IN BLOOD STREAM

MOSQUITO BITES INFECTED DOG, INGESTING MICROFILARIA

INFECTIVE LARVAE PASS TO LIPS OF MOSQUITO

MICROFILARIA MIGRATE TO MALPIGHIAN TUBES OF MOSQUITO

- - - - - DEVELOPMENT IN ONE MONTH - - - -

Heartworms were once thought to be a problem confined to the Southern part of the United States but they have become an increasingly common problem in Middle Western States. The larva is transmitted from dog to dog through the bite of the mosquito, and eight to nine months may elapse from the time the dog is bitten until the heartworm is mature. Once they have entered the bloodstream, heartworms mature in the heart, where they interfere with heart action. Symptoms include lethargy, chronic coughing, and loss of weight. Having the dog's blood examined microscopically is the only way the tiny larvae (called microfilaria) can be detected. Eradication of heartworms is extremely difficult, so a veterinarian well versed in this field should be consulted. In an area where mosquitoes are prevalent, it is well to protect the dog by keeping him in a screened-in area.

Hookworms are found in puppies as well as adult dogs. When excreted in the feces, the mature worm looks like a thread and is about three-quarters of an inch in length. Eradication is a serious problem in areas where the soil is infested with the worms, for the dog may then become reinfested after treatment. Consequently, medication usually must be repeated at intervals, and the premises—including the grounds where the dog exercises—must be treated and must be kept well drained. You may wish to consult your veterinarian regarding the vaccine for the prevention of hookworms in dogs which was licensed recently by the United States Department of Agriculture.

Roundworms are the most common of all the worms that may infest the dog, for most puppies are born with them or become infested with them shortly after birth. Roundworms vary in length from two to eight inches and can be detected readily through microscopic examination of the feces. At maturity, upon excretion, the roundworm will spiral into a circle, but after it dies it resembles a cut rubber band.

If you suspect that a puppy may have roundworms, check its gums and tongue. If the puppy is heavily infested, the worms will cause anemia and the gums and the tongue will be a very pale pink color. If the puppy is anemic, the veterinarian probably will prescribe a tonic in addition to the proper worm medicine.

Tapeworms require an intermediate host, usually the flea or the louse, but they sometimes are found in raw fish, so a dog can become infested by swallowing a flea or a louse, or by eating infested fish.

LIFE CYCLE OF THE HOOKWORM

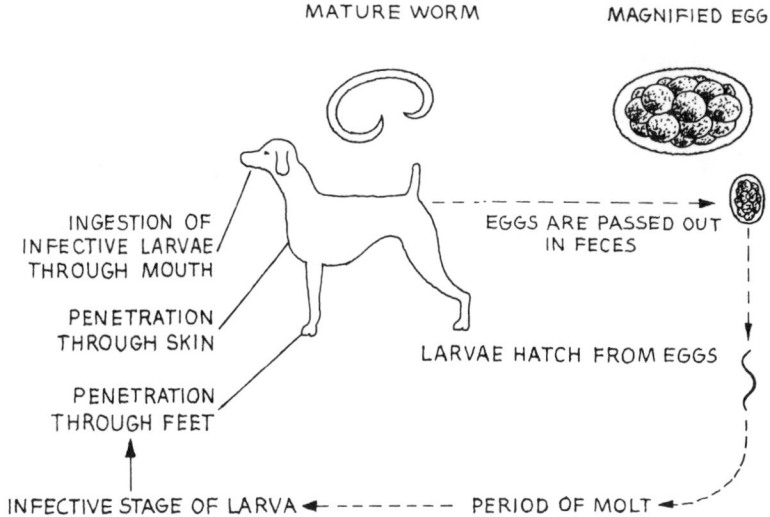

MATURE WORM

MAGNIFIED EGG

INGESTION OF
INFECTIVE LARVAE
THROUGH MOUTH

EGGS ARE PASSED OUT
IN FECES

PENETRATION
THROUGH SKIN

LARVAE HATCH FROM EGGS

PENETRATION
THROUGH FEET

INFECTIVE STAGE OF LARVA ← ─ ─ ─ ─ ─ PERIOD OF MOLT ←─ ─

LIFE CYCLE OF THE COMMON ROUNDWORM

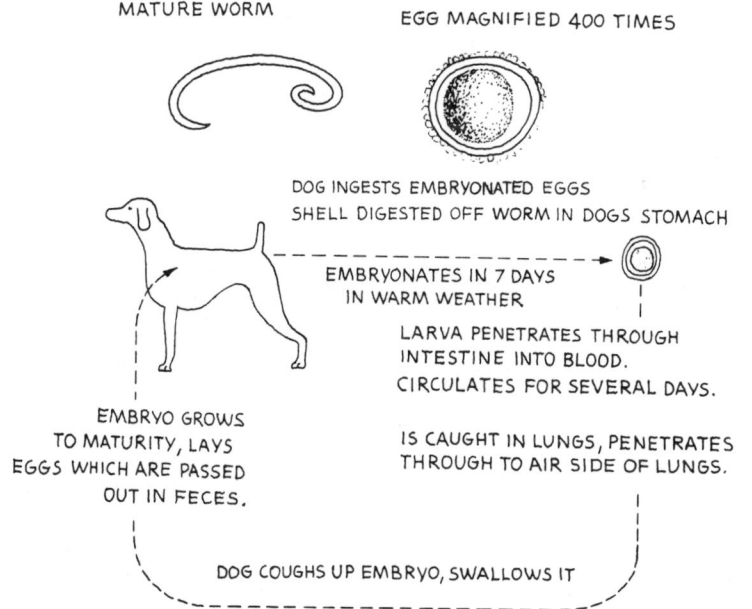

MATURE WORM

EGG MAGNIFIED 400 TIMES

DOG INGESTS EMBRYONATED EGGS
SHELL DIGESTED OFF WORM IN DOGS STOMACH

EMBRYONATES IN 7 DAYS
IN WARM WEATHER

LARVA PENETRATES THROUGH
INTESTINE INTO BLOOD.
CIRCULATES FOR SEVERAL DAYS.

EMBRYO GROWS
TO MATURITY, LAYS
EGGS WHICH ARE PASSED
OUT IN FECES.

IS CAUGHT IN LUNGS, PENETRATES
THROUGH TO AIR SIDE OF LUNGS.

DOG COUGHS UP EMBRYO, SWALLOWS IT

LIFE CYCLE OF THE FLEA-HOST TAPEWORM

MATURE WORM ———— CAPSULE WITH EGGS

DOG SWALLOWS
ADULT FLEA

MATURE PROGLOTTIDS
PASSED OFF IN FECES

FLEA MATURES

ADULT WORMS FOUND
IN SMALL INTESTINE

LARVAE EATS
PROGLOTTID

PUPA OF FLEA

FLEA LARVAE INGEST EGGS

A complete tapeworm can be two to three feet long. The head and neck of the tapeworm are small and threadlike, while the body is made up of segments like links of a sausage, which are about half an inch long and flat. Segments of the body separate from the worm and will be found in the feces or will hang from the coat around the anus and when dry will resemble dark grains of rice.

The head of the tapeworm is imbedded in the lining of the intestine where the worm feeds on the blood of the dog. The difficulty

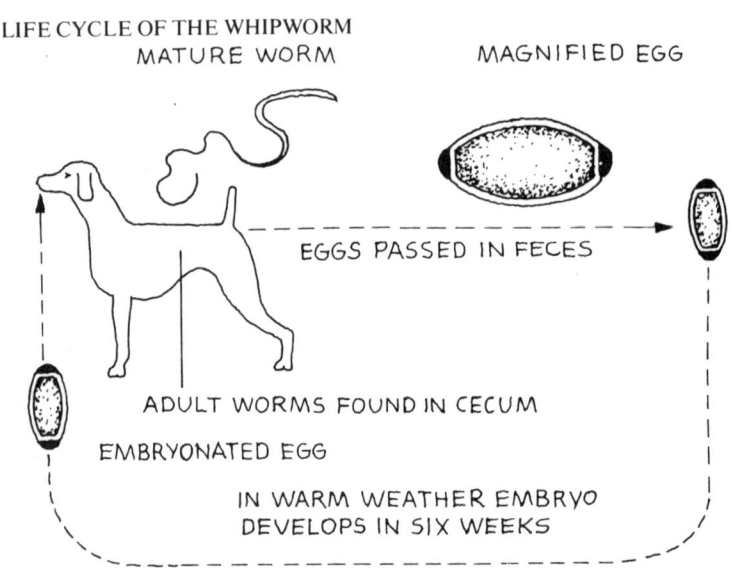

LIFE CYCLE OF THE WHIPWORM

MATURE WORM   MAGNIFIED EGG

EGGS PASSED IN FECES

ADULT WORMS FOUND IN CECUM

EMBRYONATED EGG

IN WARM WEATHER EMBRYO
DEVELOPS IN SIX WEEKS

in eradicating the tapeworm lies in the fact that most medicines have a laxative action which is too severe and which pulls the body from the head so the body is eliminated with the feces, but the implanted head remains to start growing a new body. An effective medication is a tablet which does not dissolve until it reaches the intestine where it anesthetizes the worm to loosen the head before expulsion.

Whipworms are more common in the eastern states than in states along the West Coast, but whipworms may infest dogs in any section of the United States. Whipworms vary in length from two to four inches and are tapered in shape so they resemble a buggy whip—which accounts for the name.

At maturity, the whipworm migrates into the caecum, where it is difficult to reach with medication. A fecal examination will show whether whipworms are present, so after treatment, it is best to have several examinations made in order to be sure the dog is free of them.

Skin Problems

Skin problems usually cause persistent itching. However, **follicular mange** does not usually do so but is evidenced by moth-eaten-looking patches, especially about the head and along the back. **Sarcoptic mange** produces severe itching and is evidenced by patchy, crusty areas on body, legs, and abdomen. Any evidence suggesting either should be called to the attention of a veterinarian. Both require extensive treatment and both may be contracted by humans.

Allergies are not readily distinguished from other skin troubles except through laboratory tests. However, dog owners should be alert to the fact that various coat dressings and shampoos, or simply bathing the dog too often, may produce allergic skin reactions.

Eczema is characterized by extreme itching, redness of the skin and exudation of serous matter. It may result from a variety of causes, and the exact cause in a particular case may be difficult to determine. Relief may be secured by dusting the dog twice a week with a soothing powder containing a fungicide and an insecticide.

Other Health Problems

Clogged anal glands cause intense discomfort, which the dog may attempt to relieve by scooting himself along the floor on his haunches. These glands, located on either side of the anus, se-

53

crete a substance that enables the dog to expel the contents of the rectum. If they become clogged, they may give the dog an unpleasant odor and when neglected, serious infection may result. Contents of the glands can be easily expelled into a wad of cotton, which should be held under the tail with the left hand. Then, using the right hand, pressure should be exerted with the thumb on one side of the anus, the forefinger on the other. The normal secretion is brownish in color, with an unpleasant odor. The presence of blood or pus indicates infection and should be called to the attention of a veterinarian.

Eye problems of a minor nature—redness or occasional discharge—may be treated with a few drops of boric acid solution (2%) or salt solution (1 teaspoonful table salt to 1 pint sterile water). Cuts on the eyeball, bruises close to the eyes, or persistent discharge should be treated only by a veterinarian.

Heat exhaustion is a serious (and often fatal) problem caused by exposure to extreme heat. Usually it occurs when a thoughtless owner leaves the dog in a closed vehicle without proper shade and ventilation. Even on a day when outside temperatures do not seem excessively high, heat builds up rapidly to an extremely high temperature in a closed vehicle parked in direct sunlight or even in partial shade. Many dogs and young children die each year from being left in an inadequately ventilated vehicle. To prevent such a tragedy, an owner or parent should never leave a dog or child unattended in a vehicle even for a short time.

During hot weather, whenever a dog is taken for a ride in an air-conditioned automobile, the cool air should be reduced gradually when nearing the destination, for the sudden shock of going from cool air to extremely hot temperatures can also result in shock and heat exhaustion.

Symptoms of heat exhaustion include rapid and difficult breathing and near or complete collapse. After removing the victim from the vehicle, first aid treatment consists of sponging cool water over the body to reduce temperature as quickly as possible. Immediate medical treatment is essential in severe cases of heat exhaustion.

Care of the Ailing or Injured Dog

A dog that is seriously ill, requiring surgical treatment, transfusions, or intravenous feeding, must be hospitalized. One requiring less complicated treatment is better cared for at home, but it is essential that the dog be kept in a quiet environment. Preferably his bed should be in a room apart from family activity, yet close at hand, so his condition can be checked frequently. Clean bedding and adequate warmth are essential, as are a constant supply of fresh, cool water, and foods to tempt the appetite.

Special equipment is not ordinarily needed, but the following items will be useful in caring for a sick dog, as well as in giving first aid for injuries:

petroleum jelly	tincture of metaphen
rubbing alcohol	cotton, gauze, and adhesive tape
mineral oil	burn ointment
rectal thermometer	tweezers
hydrogen peroxide	boric acid solution (2%)

If special medication is prescribed, it may be administered in any one of several ways. A pill or small capsule may be concealed in a small piece of meat, which the dog will usually swallow with no problem. A large capsule may be given by holding the dog's mouth open, inserting the capsule as far as possible down the throat, then holding the mouth closed until the dog swallows. Liquid medicine should be measured into a small bottle or test tube. Then, if the corner of the dog's lip is pulled out while the head is tilted upward, the liquid can be poured between the lips and teeth, a small amount at a time. If he refuses to swallow, keeping the dog's head tilted and stroking his throat will usually induce swallowing.

Liquid medication may also be given by use of a hypodermic syringe without a needle. The syringe is slipped into the side of the mouth and over the rise at the back of the tongue, and the medicine is "injected" slowly down the throat. This is especially good for medicine with a bad taste, for the medicine does not touch the taste buds in the front part of the tongue. It also eliminates spills and guarantees that all the medicine goes in.

Foods offered the sick dog should be particularly nutritious and easily digested. Meals should be smaller than usual and offered at more frequent intervals. If the dog is reluctant to eat, offer food he particularly likes and warm it slightly to increase aroma and thus make it more tempting.

The Stone-Age Dog.

A Spotted Dog from India, ``Parent of the modern Coach Dog.''

History of the Genus Canis

The history of man's association with the dog is a fascinating one, extending into the past at least seventy centuries, and involving the entire history of civilized man from the early Stone Age to the present.

The dog, technically a member of the genus *Canis*, belongs to the zoological family group *Canidae*, which also includes such animals as wolves, foxes, jackals, and coyotes. In the past it was generally agreed that the dog resulted from the crossing of various members of the family *Canidae*. Recent findings have amended this theory somewhat, and most authorities now feel the jackal probably has no direct relationship with the dog. Some believe dogs are descended from wolves and foxes, with the wolf the main progenitor. As evidence, they cite the fact that the teeth of the wolf are identical in every detail with those of the dog, whereas the teeth of the jackal are totally different.

Still other authorities insist that the dog always has existed as a separate and distinct animal. This group admits that it is possible for a dog to mate with a fox, coyote, or wolf, but points out that the resulting puppies are unable to breed with each other, although they can breed with stock of the same genus as either parent. Therefore, they insist, it was impossible for a new and distinct genus to have developed from such crossings. They then cite the fact that any dog can be mated with any other dog and the progeny bred among themselves. These researchers point out, too, heritable characteristics that are different in these animals. For instance, the pupil of the eye of the fox is eliptical and vertical, while the pupil is round in the dog, wolf, and coyote. Tails, too, differ considerably, for tails of foxes, coyotes, and wolves always drop behind them, while those of dogs may be carried over the back or straight up.

Much conjecture centers on two wild dog species that still exist—the Dingo of Australia, and the Dhole in India. Similar in appearance, both are reddish in color, both have rather long, slender jaws, both have rounded ears that stand straight up, and both species hunt in packs. Evidence indicates that they had the same ancestors. Yet, today, they live in areas that are more than 4,000 miles apart.

Despite the fact that it is impossible to determine just when the dog first appeared as a distinct species, archeologists have found definite proof that the dog was the first animal domesticated by man. When man lived by tracking, trapping, and killing game, the dog added to the forces through which man discovered and captured the quarry. Man shared his primitive living quarters with the dog, and the two together devoured the prey. Thus, each helped to sustain the life of the other. The dog assisted man, too, by defending the campsite against marauders. As man gradually became civilized, the dog's usefulness was extended to guarding the other animals man domesticated, and, even before the wheel was invented, the dog served as a beast of burden. In fact, archeological findings show that aboriginal peoples of Switzerland and Ireland used the dog for such purposes long before they learned to till the soil.

Cave drawings from the palaeolithic era, which was the earliest part of the Old World Stone Age, include hunting scenes in which a rough, canine-like form is shown alongside huntsmen. One of these drawings is believed to be 50,000 years old, and gives credence to the theory that all dogs are descended from a primitive type ancestor that was neither fox nor wolf.

Archeological findings show that Europeans of the New Stone Age possessed a breed of dogs of wolf-like appearance, and a similar breed has been traced through the successive Bronze Age and Iron Age. Accurate details are not available, though, as to the external appearance of domesticated dogs prior to historic times (roughly four to five thousand years ago).

Early records in Chaldean and Egyptian tombs show that several distinct and well-established dog types had been developed by about 3700 B.C. Similar records show that the early people of the Nile Valley regarded the dog as a god, often burying it as a mummy in special cemeteries and mourning its death.

Some of the early Egyptian dogs had been given names, such as Akna, Tarn, and Abu, and slender dogs of the Greyhound type and a short-legged Terrier type are depicted in drawings found in Egyptian royal tombs that are at least 5,000 years old. The Afghan Hound and the Saluki are shown in drawings of only slightly later times. Another type of ancient Egyptian dog was much heavier and more powerful, with short coat and massive head. These

58

Bas-relief of Hunters with Nets and Mastiffs. From the walls of Assurbanipal's palace at Nineveh 668-626 B.C. *British Museum.*

probably hunted by scent, as did still another type of Egyptian dog that had a thick furry coat, a tail curled almost flat over the back, and erect "prick" ears.

Early Romans and Greeks mentioned their dogs often in literature, and both made distinctions between those that hunted by sight and those that hunted by scent. The Romans' canine classifications were similar to those we use now. In addition to dogs comparable to the Greek sight and scent hounds, the ancient Romans had Canes *villatici* (housedogs) and Canes *pastorales* (sheepdogs), corresponding to our present-day working dogs.

The dog is mentioned many times in the Old Testament. The first reference, in Genesis, leads some Biblical scholars to assert that man and dog have been companions from the time man was created. And later Biblical references bring an awareness of the diversity in breeds and types existing thousands of years ago.

As civilization advanced, man found new uses for dogs. Some required great size and strength. Others needed less of these characteristics but greater agility and better sight. Still others needed an accentuated sense of smell. As time went on, men kept those puppies that suited specific purposes especially well and bred them together. Through ensuing generations of selective breeding, desirable characteristics appeared with increasing frequency. Dogs used in a particular region for a special purpose gradually became more like each other, yet less like dogs of other areas used for different purposes. Thus were established the foundations for the various breeds we have today.

The American Kennel Club, the leading dog organization in the United States, divides the various breeds into six "Groups," based on similarity of purposes for which they were developed.

"Sporting Dogs" include the Pointers, Setters, Spaniels, and Retrievers that were developed by sportsmen interested in hunting game birds. Most of the Pointers and Setters are of comparatively recent origin. Their development parallels the development of sporting firearms, and most of them evolved in the British Isles. Exceptions are the Weimaraner, which was developed in Germany, and the Vizsla, or Hungarian Pointer, believed to have been developed by the Magyar hordes that swarmed over Central Europe a

Bas-relief of Assyrian Mastiffs hunting wild horses. *British Museum.*

thousand years ago. The Irish were among the first to use Spaniels, though the name indicates that the original stock may have come from Spain. Two Sporting breeds, the American Water Spaniel and the Chesapeake Bay Retriever, were developed entirely in the United States.

"Hounds," among which are Dachshunds, Beagles, Bassets, Harriers, and Foxhounds, are used singly, in pairs, or in packs to "course" (or run) and hunt for rabbits, foxes, and various rodents. But little larger, the Norwegian Elkhound is used in its native country to hunt big game—moose, bear, and deer.

The smaller Hound breeds hunt by scent, while the Irish Wolfhound, Borzoi, Scottish Deerhound, Saluki, and Greyhound hunt by sight. The Whippet, Saluki, and Greyhound are notably fleet of foot, and racing these breeds (particularly the Greyhound) is popular sport.

The Bloodhound is a member of the Hound Group that is known world-wide for its scenting ability. On the other hand, the Basenji is a comparatively rare Hound breed and has the distinction of being the only dog that cannot bark.

"Working Dogs" have the greatest utilitarian value of all modern dogs and contribute to man's welfare in diverse ways. The Boxer, Doberman Pinscher, Rottweiler, German Shepherd, Great Dane, and Giant Schnauzer are often trained to serve as sentries and aid police in patrolling streets. The German Shepherd is especially noted as a guide dog for the blind. The Collie, the various breeds of Sheepdogs, and the two Corgi breeds are known throughout the world for their extraordinary herding ability. And the exploits of the St. Bernard and Newfoundland are legendary, their records for saving lives unsurpassed.

The Siberian Husky, the Samoyed, and the Alaskan Malamute are noted for tremendous strength and stamina. Had it not been for these hardy Northern breeds, the great polar expeditions might never have taken place, for Admiral Byrd used these dogs to reach points inaccessible by other means. Even today, with our jet-age transportation, the Northern breeds provide a more practical means of travel in frigid areas than do modern machines.

"Terriers" derive their name from the Latin *terra,* meaning "earth," for all of the breeds in this Group are fond of burrowing. Terriers hunt by digging into the earth to rout rodents and fur-bearing animals such as badgers, woodchucks, and otters. Some breeds are expected merely to force the animals from their dens in

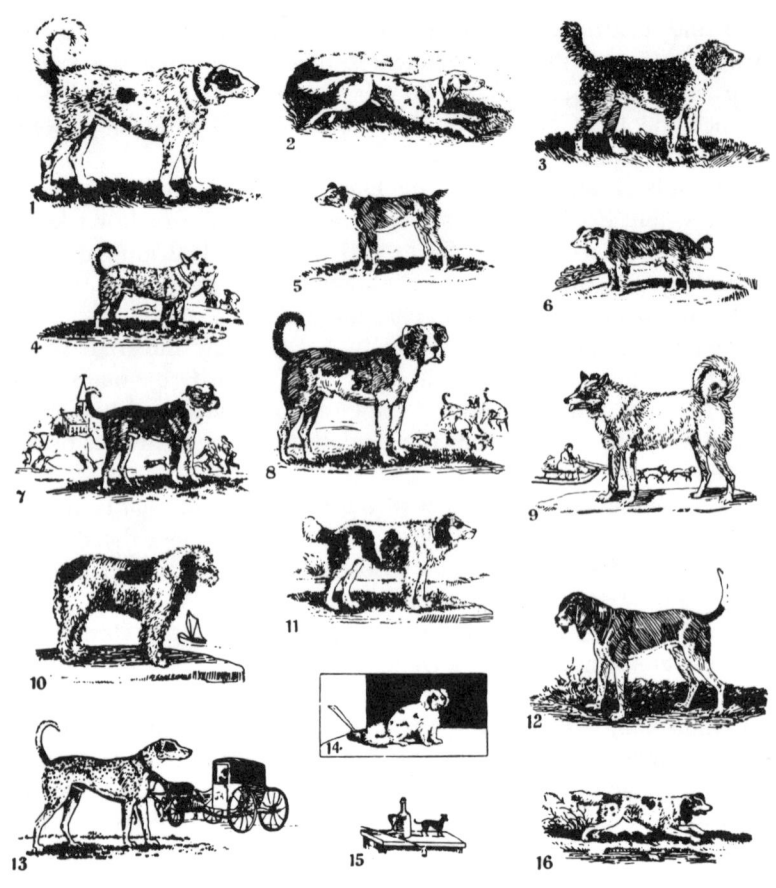

1. The Newfoundland. 2. The English Setter. 3. The Large Water-spaniel. 4. The Terrier. 5. The Cur-dog. 6. The Shepherd's Dog. 7. The Bulldog. 8. The Mastiff. 9. The Greenland Dog. 10. The Rough Water-dog. 11. The Small Water-spaniel. 12. The Old English Hound. 13. The Dalmatian or Coach-dog. 14. The Comporter (very much of a Papillon). 15. "Toy Dog, Bottle, Glass, and Pipe." *From a vignette*. 16. The Springer or Cocker. *From Thomas Bewick's "General History of Quadrupeds" (1790)*.

order that the hunter can complete the capture. Others are expected to find and destroy the prey, either on the surface or under the ground.

Terriers come in a wide variety of sizes, ranging from such large breeds as the Airedale and Kerry Blue to such small ones as the Skye, the Dandie Dinmont, the West Highland White, and the Scottish Terrier. England, Ireland, and Scotland produced most of the Terrier breeds, although the Miniature Schnauzer was developed in Germany.

"Toys," as the term indicates, are small breeds. Although they make little claim to usefulness other than as ideal housepets, Toy dogs develop as much protective instinct as do larger breeds and serve effectively in warning of the approach of strangers.

Origins of the Toys are varied. The Pekingese was developed as the royal dog of China more than two thousand years before the birth of Christ. The Chihuahua, smallest of the Toys, originated in Mexico and is believed to be a descendant of the Techichi, a dog of great religious significance to the Aztecs, while the Italian Greyhound was popular in the days of ancient Pompeii.

"Non-Sporting Dogs" include a number of popular breeds of varying ancestry. The Standard and Miniature Poodles were developed in France for the purpose of retrieving game from water. The Bulldog originated in Great Britain and was bred for the purpose of "baiting" bulls. The Chow Chow apparently originated centuries ago in China, for it is pictured in a bas relief dated to the Han dynasty of about 150 B.C.

The Dalmatian served as a carriage dog in Dalmatia, protecting travelers in bandit-infested regions. The Keeshond, recognized as the national dog of Holland, is believed to have originated in the Arctic or possibly the Sub-Arctic. The Schipperke, sometimes erroneously described as a Dutch dog, originated in the Flemish provinces of Belgium. And the Lhasa Apso came from Tibet, where it is known as "Abso Seng Kye," the "Bark Lion Sentinel Dog."

During the thousands of years that man and dog have been closely associated, a strong affinity has been built up between the two. The dog has more than earned his way as a helper, and his faithful, selfless devotion to man is legendary. The ways in which the dog has proved his intelligence, his courage, and his dependability in situations of stress are amply recorded in the countless tales of canine heroism that highlight the pages of history, both past and present.

Dogs in Woodcuts. (*1st row*) (LEFT) "Maltese dog with shorter hair";
(RIGHT) "Spotted sporting dog trained to catch game"; (*2nd row*) (LEFT)
Sporting white dog; (RIGHT) "Spanish dog with floppy ears": (*3rd row*)
(LEFT) "French dog"; (RIGHT) "Mad dog of Grevinus"; (*4th row*) (LEFT)
Hairy Maltese dog; (RIGHT) "English fighting dog . . . of horrid aspect." *From
Aldrovandus (1637).*

History of the Welsh Corgi

It is difficult if not impossible to establish an exact date for the emergence of the Welsh Corgi as a distinct type of dog. It cannot even be determined that the modern Welsh Corgi is the sole product of the British Isles. Breeds that have been created in the last one hundred to two hundred years are relatively easy to trace because of the conscientious record keeping by breeders. This is not, however, the case with the Welsh Corgi and other ancient breeds that have gone through centuries of evolution to become the purebred dogs that exist today.

The Welsh Corgi type has existed for centuries. There is evidence of the early existence of the Corgi-type dog both in literature and in art, and paintings and sculptures frequently serve to establish historical authenticity in the absence of written proof.

Many dogs that are today associated with the northern countries trace their origin back to central Europe. This only seems natural, for dogs living in a wild or semi-domesticated state would find the climate of central Europe more amenable and would be able to survive and multiply there. When these same dogs were transported to northern climates, they would need some help and protection from man in order to survive.

All modern domestic breeds trace back to four categories of dogs: the Dingo group, the northern group, the Greyhound group, and the Mastiff group. The Corgi belongs to the northern group. Others included in this group are the Northern Wolf, the Huskie, the Pomeranian, the Elkhound, the Collie, the Spitz, the Schipperke, and most Terriers.

Small domesticated hunting dogs appeared centuries before the birth of Christ in the lands at the eastern end of the Mediterranean, according to Greek writings of Xenophon in the fourth century B.C. In *Cynegeticus,* a treatise on the hunting of hare, wild boar, and deer, he refers to the small hunting dogs of the period.

References to these small dogs were frequent in both Greek and Roman literature for several centuries. The Romans divided dogs

Ch. Larklain's Red Desaster, a Best-in-Show Envoy son who was owned by Robert B. Hurst.

Ch. Larklain's Redcoat, a Best-in-Show Envoy son who was owned by Bobbie Smith.

into six different categories according to their value to man. The divisions were: Fighting Dogs *(Pugnaces)*, Scent Dogs *(Nares Sagaces)*, Coursing Sight Dogs *(Pedibus Celeres)*, Hunting Dogs *(Venatici)*, Herding Dogs *(Pastorales)*, and House Dogs *(Villatici)*.

The early ancestors of the Corgi would have come from the Hunting-Herding Dogs and were probably carried north across Europe by traveling huntsmen. The small dogs were used on small game, allowing the larger dogs to pursue such large animals as wild boar, deer, and bear. That these dogs should be brought to the British Isles seems only natural, for the islands abounded with small game, especially rabbits.

W. Lloyd-Thomas of Llanrhystyd, Cardiganshire, South Wales, is the semi-official historian of the Corgi. He has spent many years studying the little herding dog of his native Cardiganshire region of the British Isles, and indicates that the Corgi-type dog was first brought to England by the Celts some three thousand years ago. It was, rather, the pre-Celtic tribes that came to England during this period—the Urn Field people who lived in central Europe during the late Bronze Age and were the ancestors of the Celts. Their dialect served as a base for the Celtic language which was to develop at a later date.

The word Corgi is said to be derived from the Celtic words *cor* meaning *dwarf* and *gi* meaning *dog*. The plural is *corgwn*. In Welsh the words meaning *dwarf* and *dog* are *corr* and *ci*. Studies indicate that the word *corgi* became corrupted to *curgi* and was finally shortened to *cur,* which meant any non-royal dog and was commonly used to refer to all dogs owned by non-Norman Britons.

One group of these European invaders settled in South Wales in the village of Bronant in Cardiganshire, bringing their Corgi-type dogs with them, which led to the name Cardiganshire Corgi being applied to the dogs. At a much later date the name was shortened somewhat and the word Welsh was included in front of Corgi.

In the year 920 A.D., Howell Dda, King of Wales, undertook the formalizing of existing customs and practices, and in so doing established a system of laws in Wales. One such law refers to the Welsh cattle dog, which indicates the importance of this little animal in the lives of the farmers of the day. There are early references to this Welsh "heeler" as the CiSawdl.

The conversion of the little dog into a basic herding dog was the contribution of the Welsh people, for there are indications that the dog was used for hunting before being brought to the British Isles and that he had also served as a guard dog.

67

Gwen L. Platt romping in the fields of Maine with four of her Rojan Way Pembroke Welsh Corgis.

The early specimens of the breed were undoubtedly the result of breedings between the wild wolf and the Spitz-type dog, a semi-domesticated type found throughout the mid-sections of Europe and western Asia. Some evidence has also been advanced that there are certain similarities to the Dachshund and to the German Basset, especially in the lowness to the ground and the bone structure of the legs. Some reference has even been made to the Egyptian Tesem.

The provinces of South Wales are well isolated from each other and communication and transportation between provinces were difficult because of the Cambrian Mountains. This would explain why the early Corgi, once introduced into South Wales, developed easily into a distinct breed. New blood was not likely to have been introduced, thus leading to an unstructured program of inbreeding.

The Pembroke-type Corgi was a different breed entirely from the Cardigan. Henry I of England is credited with the introduction of this breed. In 1107, in an effort to bring a new trade to the country, the king brought over a colony of Flemish weavers. When they came they brought with them their small herding-guard dogs. These dogs enjoyed a degree of popularity—especially so when Henry II acquired one of his own. While some historians say the Flemish weavers eventually established a colony in the province of Pembrokeshire in South Wales, a number of authorities are no longer willing to accept this explanation, citing a lack of Flemish traditions in the customs of the area, which they feel discounts this theory.

The Pembroke Welsh Corgi traces its origin in a somewhat different way back to the early wolf-line ancestors. The Pembroke is said to trace back to the Keeshond, the Samoyed, the Schipperke, and the Norwegian Elkhound. The Västgötaspets, native to Sweden, is not, according to some historians, related directly to the Pembroke Welsh Corgi unless it is the ancestor of the Corgi. But the invasions of Wales by the Vikings in the ninth and tenth centuries could easily explain the introduction of the Västgötaspets into this region, and one has only to look at pictures of the two dogs to see the strong resemblance between them. The Västgötaspets is in the same weight category but stands between thirteen and sixteen inches at the withers and has a tail up to four inches long. The Corgi in the early twentieth century was well within the lower limits of this height range, reaching up to fourteen inches at the withers.

The Cardigan Welsh Corgi is said to be more closely related to

69

the Swedish Vallhund or the Norwegian Buhund, which are also of Celtic origin. Some authorities believe that the small Spitz-type dogs were brought to Wales from Scandinavia by the Vikings and were originally used as guard dogs for the house rather than as herding dogs.

The Welsh did distinguish between the two breeds almost from the beginning, using descriptive titles for each. The Pembroke was called Ci Soldi, which means *heeling dog,* while the Cardigan was called Ci Llathaid, or the *meter-long dog.* This does tend to prove that from the beginning the two were distinct and separate breeds.

Sixteenth century British law forbade poaching on the large areas of land belonging to the crown, which undoubtedly worked great hardships on the lower classes of the day. Some slight exceptions were made, however, from time to time. The king, who was basically interested in the hunting of large game, especially the stag, would hunt rabbits occasionally, though that was certainly not his favorite sport. Considering the prolificness of the rabbit, it is easy to understand why some relaxing of controls would be needed to keep the rabbit population down, and allowing small dogs to hunt on these lands occasionally would serve as the necessary control. A too-careful protection of the rabbit population would disturb the necessary balance of nature and might even threaten the deer population.

The closing of the crown lands tended to deter the increase in Corgi population by eliminating the hunting need for the dog. As a result, the Corgi was used almost exclusively for herding cattle during the seventeenth and eighteenth centuries. With the change in emphasis during the nineteenth century, and an increased interest in the raising of sheep, the need for a different type of Corgi was felt.

The mouth of the Cardigan used for cattle herding was a little too rough for the herding of sheep, for it was not necessary for the dog to nip at the hoofs of the sheep to control them. To convert the dog and to modify the mouth, the Welsh crossed the Cardigans with the Welsh Collies. This not only brought about the sought-after change, but also brought in other modifications in the dog, including changes in both the texture and the quantity of coat.

With the improvement of transportation and communication during the early part of the twentieth century, the isolation of Cardiganshire and Pembrokeshire began to diminish. This resulted in some Cardigan Welsh Corgis' being brought to Pembrokeshire, where they were crossed with the Pembrokes. It is interesting to

American and Brazilian Ch. Larklain's Tarter, multiple Group winner owned by Elaine P. Erganbright.

note that there are frequent references of the Cardigan blood's being introduced into the Pembroke, but a complete lack of evidence of the Pembroke blood's being introduced into the Cardigan.

While interest in purebred dogs had been formalized as early as 1873 with the founding of the English Kennel Club, it was not until 1925 that the Welsh Corgi Club was established in England. In spite of its name, this club was limited to the Pembroke. Breeders of the Cardigan established their own society in 1926, the Cardigan Welsh Corgi Association.

Pembroke Corgis were first exhibited at local agricultural shows in the 1890s in Wales. These were, of course, not shows sanctioned by the English Kennel Club. It was not until 1927 that Crufts established separate classes for the Cardigan and the Pembroke. In 1928 the Corgi was accepted for registration by the English Kennel Club and the first Challenge Certificate was awarded at the Cardiff show that same year.

During the late 1920s, some interest was expressed in the Corgi by dog lovers in the United States. As a result, some Corgis were imported by Americans every year, with the number gradually increasing until the start of World War II.

The English Kennel Club accepted the Standards for the Cardigan Welsh Corgi and the Pembroke Welsh Corgi in 1923. Ever since that date the two have been kept as separate breeds rather than as one breed or as two varieties of a single breed. The Pembroke Welsh Corgi gained new interest and importance in 1936 when King George VI gave Rozavel Golden Eagle to his daughter Princess Elizabeth, who is now Queen of England.

The interest of English breeders continued in both breeds and reached a peak for the Cardigan Welsh Corgi in 1959 with a registration of 371. In 1960 the registrations for the Pembroke Welsh Corgi peaked with a registration of 8,933. Registrations are running at about half these numbers today.

Ch. Bundocks Apple of the Eye, owned by Douglas and Gladys Bundock.

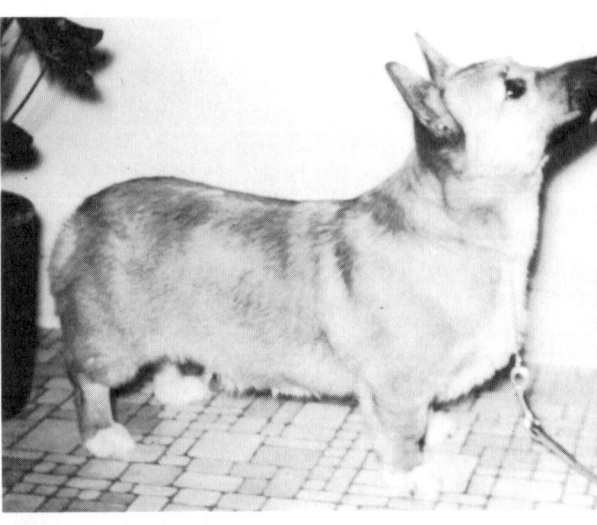

Ch. Red Envoy of Brome, CD, at six months of age. The leading Pembroke Welsh Corgi sire, with fifty-two champion get, Envoy was imported from England by Elaine P. Erganbright.

Ch. Larklain's Firebright, a Best-in-Show Envoy son who was owned by Robert B. Hurst.

The Welsh Corgi in the United States

In 1976 The American Kennel Club registered 1,048,648 individual dogs of some one hundred twenty-two breeds of purebred dogs. The Cardigan Welsh Corgi ranked eighty-eighth in popularity with an annual registration of 356 and the Pembroke Welsh Corgi ranked forty-eighth with 2061 registrations. Most Corgi breeders are pleased that the two breeds are no more popular than they are. Since the demand for Corgis is not as great as the demand for a number of other breeds, commercial kennels have not entered the field and bred indiscriminately. This has helped to maintain a certain purity in the breeds and has maintained a definite strength of bloodlines. It is hoped that the breeds' popularity does not spread beyond the dedicated Corgiophiles.

The following charts show the numbers of Corgis that were registered during an eight-year period from 1969 through 1976.

Cardigan Welsh Corgi

	1969	1970	1971	1972	1973	1974	1975	1976
January	21	19	32	31	38	36	46	25
February	23	31	32	27	39	28	29	31
March	25	20	36	28	46	25	24	41
April	32	26	43	41	34	36	44	47
May	29	28	29	38	28	12	30	26
June	27	22	31	18	27	20	27	35
July	27	20	18	27	29	21	30	28
August	44	25	25	40	48	42	21	24
September	33	25	23	37	21	18	35	17
October	27	33	31	25	30	33	31	25
November	17	25	42	36	26	29	20	28
December	19	20	18	24	20	25	32	29
	324	294	332	372	383	325	369	356

73

Ch. Foxshire Achilles, owned by Ernest and Suzanne Mann.

Pembroke Welsh Corgi

	1969	1970	1971	1972	1973	1974	1975	1976
January	177	217	185	192	211	242	166	157
February	217	222	219	184	204	187	183	162
March	217	249	240	209	222	225	147	231
April	199	253	206	227	198	221	172	181
May	174	216	192	189	179	205	127	134
June	140	242	252	150	170	181	184	169
July	152	177	193	177	205	211	143	155
August	177	161	187	185	239	210	159	205
September	167	159	175	199	177	179	203	158
October	195	177	191	204	181	206	156	206
November	150	206	161	191	169	150	131	163
December	196	167	153	149	135	157	136	141
	2,161	2,446	2,354	2,256	2,290	2,374	1,907	2,061

In 1976 sixty-eight Cardigans earned their championships, or 19 percent compared to total registrations that year, while 131 Pembrokes finished for 6.3 percent of the registrants. This does not mean that the dogs were registered and finished in the same year, but it does serve to give a general comparison of ratios between the two breeds and their total registrations.

There are many kennels that breed and show Welsh Corgis today, and still others that were once prominent but are no longer operating. The kennels that have been selected to be included in this chapter are those that have been most active in the ten- to fifteen-year period. The listing is in alphabetical order according to kennel prefix.

Barkoy Kennel was established in 1962 by Yvonne Kollar and is located in Huntington Station, New York. American and Canadian Ch. Cleden's Paper Tiger of Barkoy has served as the foundation stud and figures in the pedigrees of many of the dogs bred here. Other Pembrokes bred or owned by the kennel are American and Canadian Ch. Crowd Pleaser of Barkoy, Ch. Money Maker of Barkoy, American and Canadian Ch. Mackson Souvenier of Kitch, and Ch. Cote de Neige Station Break. In addition to Welsh Corgis, Barkoy also raises German Shepherds.

Bear Acres Kennel of Mrs. Stanley Bear is located in San Jose, California. The Pembroke foundation stock was obtained from Cote de Neige Kennel and included such winners as Ch. Cote de Neige Red Flag, Ch. Cote de Neige Apron Strings, and Ch. Cote de

Neige Quaker Square Cu. These dogs figure in the pedigrees of Ch. Bear Acres One for the Money, Ch. Bear Acres Two Timer, Ch. Bear Acres Shoe Strings, and Ch. Bear Acres Country Cousin. Ch. Bear Acres Two for the Road is the sire of the Best-in-Show winning Ch. Bear Acres Mister Snowshoes, owned by Mrs. Frank Hayward of Ross, California, and Ch. Larklain Spain of Bear Acres, owned by the Author.

Ch. Twinroc Caesar's Cadet, owned by Paul and Doris Slaboda.

Bouev's Cardigan Kennel, owned by Arthur R. Boulanger and William C. Evans, was established in 1970 and is located in Centreville, Virginia. The foundation stock was obtained from the Brymore and Swansea Kennels and produced such winners as Ch. Bouev's Ebony Checkmate and Ch. Bouev's Rubicon Sweet Sue. Brymore Kennel is co-owned by Mrs. Michael Pym and Mrs. Henning Nelms of Oakton, Virginia. This Cardigan kennel was established in 1961 with foundation stock imported from the Kentwood and Parmel Kennels in England. Among these imports were Ch. Parmel Bryn, Ch. Kentwood Eirowyn and Ch. Kentwood Betsan, and Ch. Parmel Dictator. A number of Brymore champions have been finished by the home kennel as well as by new owners who purchased stock from Brymore. Among them are Ch. Brymore's Mr. Lucky Ap Cymmie, Ch. Brymore's Beau Geste, owned by Rollingwood Kennel, Ch. Brymore's Gawaine, and Ch. Brymore's Taliesin, the Westminster Best-of-Breed winner. In addition to Cardigans, Brymore is actively engaged in breeding Japanese Spaniels. The kennel has also actively campaigned Doberman Pinschers, Beagles, Lhasa Apsos, and Miniature Pinschers.

Bundocks Kennel is located in Sebastopol, California, and is owned by professional handler Douglas Bundock and his wife, Gladys. This kennel has been active in breeding and showing Pembrokes since 1956. The foundation stud was the English import, American and Canadian Ch. Gladiator of Rode, American UD and Canadian CDX. Additional stock was obtained from the Rover Run Kennel of Carol Roever Simonds and Cote de Neige Kennel. Both conformation and obedience titles have been earned by several dozen dogs from this kennel. American and Canadian Ch. Bundocks Rover Run Concerto, American and Canadian UD, was Highest Scoring Dog in Trial fifteen times and was the star of the Walt Disney television film *Little Dog Lost*. Ch. Bundocks Kiss Me Kate was in a second Disney film, *City Fox*. Among the other winners are Ch. Bundocks Arch Rival, CD; Ch. Bundocks Wishing Star, CDX; Ch. Bundocks Firecracker, CDX; and Ch. Bundocks Fife 'n' Drum, CD. The Group winning Ch. Bundock-Cote de Neige Playboy is a son of American and Canadian Ch. Cote de Neige Derek, who was bred by Marjorie Butcher, campaigned by Mr. and Mrs. Clive N. Pillsbury, and handled by Douglas Bundock. He won six Best-in-Show awards and twenty-six Group Firsts. Under the Phillips System he was the Number One Corgi in 1963, 1964, and 1965. He is now owned by the Bundocks.

Ch. Foxlee Bryn Beau, owned by Charles and Ruth Lee.

Ch. Beaujangle Believes 'n Trolls, CD, owned by John and Martha Behringer.

Busy B's Kennel of Pembrokes is owned by Lynn Brooks and is located in Wisconsin Rapids, Wisconsin. An early home-bred bitch from this kennel is Ch. Busy B's Cherry Bark Key, the dam of six champions. Two of her offspring are Ch. Busy B's Bark of Flintshire, still in the kennel, and Ch. Bush B's Bark of Tydfil, who is owned by June E. Goodrich.

Ceceline Kennel is owned by Alice and Bob Sims of Augusta, Kansas. This kennel, established in 1964, raises both Cardigans and Pembrokes as well as German Shepherds. Among the Pembrokes in the kennel at present is Ch. Brix Soc-it-to-me, and among the Cardigans are the English import Ch. Robgwen Appalinarius Clem and Ch. Swansea Brynda of Ceceline.

Cote de Neige Kennel of Pembrokes in Bedford Village, New York, was owned by Marjorie Butcher. Mrs. Butcher died in 1973 but the record she established in the breed and her influence as a breeder will be felt for years. Ch. Cote de Neige Sundew, owned by Mrs. William B. Long, was Best in Show seven times and the sire of sixteen champions. Ch. Cote de Neige Derek, owned by the Bundocks, won six Best-in-Show awards. Ch. Cote de Neige Christmas Candy was the sire of twenty-two champions. Among the top-producing dams are Ch. Cote de Neige Christmas Rush, with seven champion offspring; Ch. Cote de Neige Garland, with six; and Ch. Cote de Neige Magic Flute, also with six. Ch. Cote de Neige Storm Cloud won the National Specialty in 1959; Ch. Cote de Neige Derek was Best of Breed in 1965; Ch. Cote de Neige Dilly Dally in 1965; and Ch. Cote de Neige Pennysaver was Best of Breed in 1966 and 1967 and Best of Opposite Sex in 1972. Others going Best of Opposite Sex at the Specialties include: Ch. Cote de Neige Garland in 1958, Ch. Cote de Neige Sundew in 1959, Ch. Cote de Neige News Item in 1964, and Ch. Cote de Neige Chance of Fox Run in 1969 and 1970. Imported English stud dogs that figure in most of the pedigrees of Cote de Neige dogs are American and Bermudian Ch. Maracas Gale Force of Cleden (sire of twenty-seven champions), Ch. Stormerbanks of Cote de Neige (sire of forty champions), and English, American, and Canadian Ch. Lees Symphony (sire of twenty-six champions). Ch. Lees Symphony, owned by Mrs. J. D. Duncan, won the Specialty in 1953 and 1956, and Ch. Maracas Gale Force of Cleden was Winners Dog in 1956 and Best of Breed in 1958. He was owned by L. C. Cleland.

Cottleston Pembroke Kennel is owned by professional handler Ruth Cooper and James Mitchel of Glenview, Illinois. Winners include Ch. Cottleston Croquet, Ch. Cottleston Cricket, and Ch.

Pera Pwysi, CDX, owned by Raymond and Margaret C. Hickel.

American and Mexican Ch. Pera Brigwyn Blue, UDT, Mexican PCE, owned by John and Helen Cramer.

Ch. Katydid's Bronz Hutch, male Pembroke, owned by Mr. and Mrs. James C. Falkner.

Cottleston Calico. Calico and Cricket are owned by the Ernest Manns.

Dorre Don Kennel, owned by John and Helen Cramer of Spring Valley, California, was established to breed German Shepherds in 1949 and has bred Cardigans since 1969. The foundation stud was American and Mexican Ch. Pera Brigwyn Blue, UDT, PCE. The bitch Ch. Dorre Don Serchus of Winsdon, UD, PC, is the dam of six champions. Their daughter Ch. Dorre Don's Blue Tango, UD, PC, was top obedience Cardigan in 1973 as her father had been in 1970, 1971, and 1972. Other winners from this kennel are Ch. Dorre Don's Incorrigible, CD, owned by the Herberts; Ch. Dorre Don's Fiddles DD of TP, owned by the Rocchios; and Ch. Hedline's Nan of Dorre Don, CD, owned by Theodore Sprague.

Emlyn Pembrokes Kennel was established in Englewood, Colorado, in 1965 by Gail A. Evans. The brood bitch Ch. Her Majesty, CD, has been joined by Ch. Emlyn's Flashfire, Ch. Emlyn's Sweet Caroline, and Ch. Emlyn's Old-fashioned Girl.

Evanwhit Kennel was established in 1963 in Renton, Washington, by Barbara A. Evans. The foundation stock was imported from England and included Ch. Winsdelf Tilda of Beal Close and Ch. Winsdelf Gallant. Carrying the kennel prefix are: Ch. Evanwhit's Copper Khan, CD; Ch. Evanwhit's Fancy; Ch. Evanwhit's J. C. Super Star, co-owned with M. Marshall; and Ch. Evanwhit's Easy Lovin', owned by Ellen Gilliland.

Fox Covert Kennel was established in 1956 by Michael J. Sauve of Rockford, Michigan. Foundation breeding stock was purchased from Cote de Neige and Larklain Kennels: Ch. Cote de Neige Gold Thimble, Canadian Ch. Cote de Neige Tea and Sympathy, and American and Canadian Ch. Larklain Flurrie. Best-in-Show winning American and Canadian Ch. Cormanby Cadenza is co-owned with his breeder, Barbara B. Hedberg. A second Best-in-Show winner is American and Canadian Ch. Penbroch Ufudd, a bitch who is co-owned with Ruth Cooper of Cottleston Kennel. Other winners are Ch. Lees Travellers Joy and Ch. Stormerbanks May Girl. In addition to Pembrokes, Fox Covert breeds Pekingese, Beagles, and Miniature Poodles.

Fox-Fire Kennel of Mrs. Marge Riccardi in North Royalton, Ohio, is one of the newer Cardigan kennels. Ch. Winsdown Black Palladium is the foundation stud. Other breeding stock was obtained from Foxlee and Twinroc Kennels.

Foxlee Kennel is owned by Mr. and Mrs. Charles Lee of Springfield, Illinois. The Swansea bloodlines figure strongly in the breeding program here. A winning bitch carrying the kennel prefix is Ch. Foxlee Mari Maudee.

Foxshire Kennel was established in 1971 by Ernest and Suzanne Mann in Northbrook, Illinois. Foundation stock included Ch. Cottleston Cricket and Ch. Cottleston Calico. Home-bred Pembroke winners are Ch. Foxshire Achilles and Ch. Foxshire Applause.

Olive M. Gardiner of Los Angeles, California, does not have a breeding kennel, but she has been active in obedience work with her Pembrokes. She has Ch. Gardiner Jones, UDT, and Gardiner Djinn, CD. The bench champion dog with a Tracking degree is a rare animal. Only a very limited number of dogs have earned this distinction.

Georgian Court is the Cardigan kennel of Andrea Vrana of Schuyler, Nebraska. Breeding lines trace to Dilwell, Parmel, and Kentwood, and the foundation bitch is Ch. Lucky Lane's M'Lady Frolic, CD. The kennel also includes Rottweilers.

Glenjoy Kennel was established in 1966 by Glennis O. Miller of Churchton, Maryland. This Cardigan line traces back to Kentwood and Parmel. Among the show dogs in the kennel are Ch. Kentwood Heulog, Ch. Parmel Dirk, English and American Ch. Robgwen Welsh Fire and the Group placing Ch. Winsdown Black Dragon. They are joined by such home-bred dogs as Ch. Glenjoy's Veiled Myth, CD, Ch. Glenjoy's Blue Charm Ap Sage, and Ch. Glenjoy Winsdown Black Dian.

The Jalma Kennel of Dr. Lawrence Boersma has bred Pembrokes in South New Berlin, New York, since 1965. Ch. Cadet's Harmony of Rose Arbor, Ch. RamWood's Rusty Rocket, and Ch. Cleden's Kiss-Me-Kate of Jalma are all line-bred on Ch. Maracas Monarch of Cleden.

Larklain Kennel was established by Elaine P. Erganbright in Denver, Colorado, in 1950. This kennel has the distinction of having bred more champions and obedience title holders than any other Corgi kennel in the country. There are more than one hundred Larklain champions and more than three dozen dogs with obedience degrees. In 1958 Red Envoy of Brome was imported from Mrs. Rose Johnson of Brome Kennel in England. He easily earned his championship and his Companion Dog degree. He stamped his quality on the breed by being the all-time leading sire in Pembrokes with fifty-one champion get. Four of his offspring, Ch. Larklain's Firebright, Ch. Larklain's Emblem, Ch. Larklain's Redcoat, and Ch. Larklain's Red Desaster, went on to win Best-in-Show awards. Ch. Larklain Topper is also a leading stud with nineteen champion get. Larklain's Token is the top-producing dam with nine champions. Ch. Larklain Babeta is the dam of eight champions and Ch. Larklain's Toppy has six champion offspring. Ch. Larklain Katy-did earned the UDT, and Larklain's Tarter became an American and Brazilian champion and a multiple Group winner. In addition to finishing more than eighty home-bred champions, Mrs. Erganbright has imported many dogs from England which she has shown to championship, including the Group winning Ch. Enterprise of Brome, an Envoy half-brother, and Ch. Red Envoy's Richochet, who is also a Group winner. The current stud at the kennel is Ch. Bekoupenn Count Doronicum, CD, who is the sire of more than a dozen champions.

Llanfair Cardigan Kennel of Coatesville, Pennsylvania, is owned by Emiline Steinbronn and Ferron John. Winners carrying this prefix are Ch. Llanfair's Shandi, CD, Ch. Llanfair's Misty Blue Echo, and Ch. Llanfair's Blue Magic.

The Pemwelgi Pembroke Kennel of all-breed judge Derek G. Rayne and his wife is located in Carmel, California. Their interest in the Corgi dates back to the thirties when they purchased International Ch. Sierra Bowhit Pivot. Other great winners owned by this kennel are: Ch. Nebriowa Miss Bobbisox, a multiple Group winner; English and American Ch. Rockrose of Wey, winner of twenty-seven Group Firsts and five Best-in-Show awards; and English and American Ch. Winrod Rosana, who won four Best-in-Show awards before leaving England.

Pera Cardigans have been bred by Raymond and Margaret C. Hickel in San Fernando, California, since 1963. The foundation bitches were from the Botticher's Ap Pilgrim line and were by the English import, Ch. Parmel Dirk, a litter brother to the great English winner, English Ch. Parmel Digger. The home-bred Ch. Pera Smoke Screen Ap Keeche, CD, was the sire of American and Mexican Ch. Pera Brigwyn Blue, UDT, PCE, and Ch. Pera Tyche Indikos, CDX. Other winners include Ch. Pera Pwysi, CDX, and Ch. Pera Pila Pala, CD, who is now owned by C. Heckman and G. Langlois, Sr., of Louisiana.

Rivendell Kennel of Judy L. Mack is located in Aptos, California. This young kennel obtained its foundation stock from the Swansea Kennel. Current winners are the Group placing Ch. Merrilane's Sweet Crazy Daze and Ch. Merrilane's Sweet Foxy Lady.

The Rojan Way Pembroke Kennel of Gwen L. Platt has been in Kennebunkport, Maine, since 1959. The bloodlines from this kennel go back to Ch. Cote de Neige Sundew through his son, the all-time top-winning Ch. Willets Red Jacket. The present stud force includes Ch. Macksons the Young Pretender and Ch. Cote de Neige Fairy Tale. Other winners currently in the kennel are Ch. Rojan Way Southern Belle and Ch. Eversridge Meg of Rojan Way.

The Rollingwood Cardigan Kennel of David and Priscilla Benkin has been in Chevy Chase, Maryland, since 1968. Their foundation stud, Ch. Brymore's Beau Geste, is of Parmel-Kentwood breeding. Current title holders include Ch. Rollingwood Brymore Betsy II, Ch. Rollingwood Rus-T Dus-T Fields, and the Number One blue merle for 1973, Ch. Rollingwood's Blue Marlee.

Rover Run Kennel is owned by Carol R. Simonds of San Rafael, California. An early home-bred dog was Ch. Rover Run Minstrel Man, who won seven Group Firsts. He was a grandson of English Ch. Maracas Masterpiece and English, American, and Canadian Ch. Lees Symphony. Other winners are Ch. Rover Run Amigo and Ch. Rover Run Daily Double.

Springdale Cardigan Kennel is owned by Harold K. Nelson of Washington, D. C. Among his winners are Ch. Springdale Dilys and Ch. Springdale Droednoeth.

Swansea Cardigan Kennel is owned by Margaret S. Douglas and Pat Santi of Yadkinville, North Carolina. The Swansea prefix appears in the names of several dozen winning dogs, and many new breeders have sought their foundation stock from this kennel. Among the winners are: Ch. Swansea Prince of Rhydowen; Ch. Swansea Cariad of Glendowner, owned by the Paul Cummings; Ch. Swansea Domino Too O Dorisu, owned by Doris Freese; and Ch. Swansea Lady Beth, owned by M. Malone. Other winners are: Ch. Swansea Princess Ayn, Ch. Swansea I'm a Honey, and Ch. Swansea Red Wing.

American and Canadian Ch. Gladiator of Rode, UD, Canadian CDX, an English import who was owned by Douglas and Gladys Bundock.

Ch. Her Majesty, CD, dam of four champions, owned by Gail A. Evans.

Trafran Kennel of El Paso, Texas, is owned by Travis P. Shackelford and Joan L. Maskie. Foundation stock obtained from Larklain Kennel included Ch. Larklain's Flashy, Ch. Larklain's Drummer Boy, Ch. Larklain's Red Charge, and Ch. Larklain's Sonata. In 1970 Rozavel Field Marshall was imported from Thelma Gray of England. He finished his championship easily and became a Group winner. The current stud force includes sons of the English studs, English Ch. Kaytop Lollypop and Ch. Caswell Duskie Knight.

Troll Hill Kennel was established in 1971 in Spartanburg, South Carolina, by John and Martha Behringer. As its foundation stud, this Cardigan kennel purchased Ch. Winsdown Zephyr, CD, the Number Two Cardigan in 1973. He was joined by Ch. Beaujangles Believes'n Trolls, CD, and Ch. Brymore's Thea Ap Gawaine.

Twinroc Cardigan Kennel is owned by Paul and Doris Slaboda of Cream Ridge, New Jersey. The leading stud dog of this kennel is Ch. Twinroc Caesar's Cadet, who has placed in the Group. His

Ch. Emlyn's Sweet Caroline, co-owned by Gail A. Evans and John W. Girton, Jr.

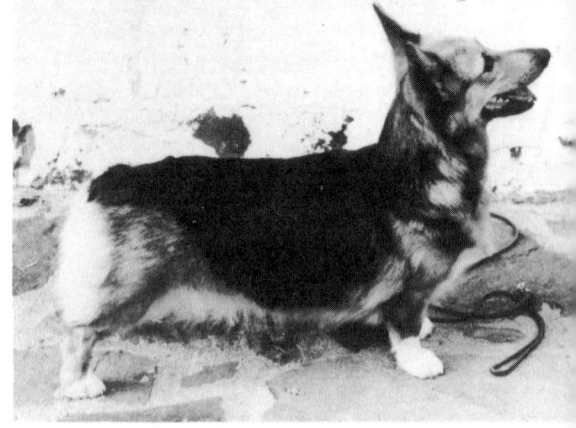

Ch. Edwina of Wark, CDX, owned by Mrs. David Wark.

Neige Sundew, who was Number Two with seven Best-in-Show awards and sixteen champion get.

Windjammer Pembroke Kennel was established in Junction City, Wisconsin, in 1970 by S. K. MacDonald, with Ch. Busy B's Scarlet Frost Fyre as the foundation stud. The first champion bitch was Ch. Sunnyband Windjammer Tart. In addition to Pembrokes, Windjammer also breeds German Shepherds.

Winsdown Cardigan Kennel, owned by Louise C. Vantrease of Lewisville, North Carolina, has been responsible for many dogs winning under the Winsdown prefix. Included in this list are Ch. Winsdown Black Dragon, owned by Glennis O. Miller and Joseph P. Kearns; Ch. Winsdown Black Bellrosa, owned by Alice Sims; Ch. Winsdown Magic Man, owned by Norma and Orren Beaty; and Ch. Winsdown Brymore Cover Girl, owned by Foxwyn. Cover Girl is the dam of five champions. A distinct honor belongs to this kennel, for Ch. Winsdown Blue Disk, bred by Louise Vantrease, was exported to England, where he completed his English championship for Mrs. Gwen Roberts of Robgwen Kennel. Winsdown imported Australian Ch. Rryde Symphony and showed him to his American and Canadian championship titles.

Ch. Dorre Don Serchus of Winsdown, UD, Mexican PC, owned by John and Helen Cramer.

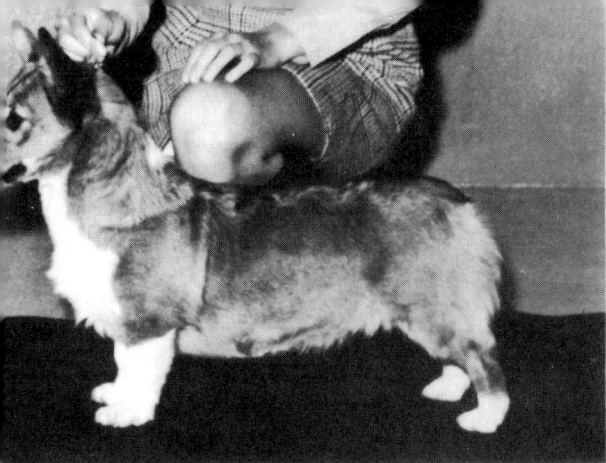

Ch. Katydid King's Lisa, CD, owned by Carole-Joy Evert.

kennel mate, Ch. Eastwyn Miss Friendly, was Best of Opposite Sex at the 1974 National Specialty.

Mrs. David Wark established her Pembroke kennel in Broken Arrow, Oklahoma, in 1962. Her first Corgi, Ch. Willow Farm Fire Fly, CD, was the dam of Ch. Dolly of Wark, CD. When Fire Fly was bred to Ch. Halmor's Winrod Spencer, she produced four champions in one litter: Ch. Edwina of Wark, CDX; Ch. Expo of Wark, CD; Ch. Emeline of Wark; and Ch. Halmor's Escapade of Wark.

Wicklow Pembroke Kennel was established in Holt, Missouri, in 1971 by Mr. and Mrs. Dennis VanVelzer. Their foundation bitch, Ch. Fox Run's All Bets Down, was bred to the English import, American and Canadian Ch. Lees Briardale Midnight and produced the tricolored Ch. Wicklow's Whizzer. Whizzer was Winners Dog at the 1972 National Specialty and has since earned a Best-in-Show award.

Willets Kennel was owned by Mrs. William B. Long of Carlisle, Massachusetts. She owned Ch. Willets Red Jacket, who holds the all-time record of eighteen Best-in-Show wins. He was also the sire of twelve champions. Mrs. Long also owned Ch. Cote de

Ch. Emeline of Wark, owned by Mrs. David Wark.

Ch. Bekonpenn Count Doronicum, CD, imported by Elaine P. Erganbright.

English Ch. Georgette of Wey, a Group winner owned by Mrs. Kenneth Butler of Surrey.

The Welsh Corgi in Other Countries

The English Kennel Club is the oldest such organization in the world with its founding date of 1873. The second oldest is The American Kennel Club, founded in 1884. In France 1884 was also the year in which the *Société d'Acclimation* was formalized into the *Société Centrale pour l'Amelioration des Races de Chiens*. This title has more recently been shortened to *Société Centrale Canine*.

Other early organizations are: the New Zealand Kennel Club, 1886; the Kennel Club of Denmark *(Dansk Kennelklub)*, 1887; the Kennel Club of Sweden *(Svenska Kennel Klubben)*, 1888; the Canadian Kennel Club, 1888; the Finnish Kennel Club *(Suomen Kennellitto-Finska Kennelklubben)*, 1889; and the Norwegian Kennel Club *(Norsk Kennel Klub)*, 1889. Other more recent clubs are: the German Kennel Club *(Verband für das Deutsche Hundewesen)*, the Spanish Central Society *(Real Sociedad Central de Fomento de las Razas Caninas en España)*; the Portuguese Kennel Club *(Clube Portuguese de Canicultura)*, and the Australian National Kennel Council established as recently as 1958. This latter organization serves as a central unit for the clubs of the various states in Australia. The Scandinavian Kennel Union founded in 1953 serves the same function for the four Scandinavian countries.

While the English Kennel Club was not established until 1873, a group of interested breeders had more or less formalized classifications of dogs as early as 1859. Dogs were divided into two categories: Sporting and Non-Sporting. This division was formalized in 1881 and continued until 1947 when Sporting was further sub-divided into Hounds, Gundogs, and Terriers. The present Group divisions in England are similar to those in the United States. They are: Hound, Gundogs, Working, Terrier, Toys, and Utility. While these divisions may correspond between the two countries, the same dogs are not necessarily in the same Groups in both countries. For example, Shih Tzus are in the Utility Group instead of the Toy Group, and Schnauzers also are in the Utility Group instead of in the Terrier and the Working Groups.

In England championship is not based on a point system as it is in the United States. Instead, the winning of three Challenge Certificates under three different judges entitles a dog to be called champion. The total number of CC's to be awarded each year is established by the English Kennel Club on a nation-wide basis, while the number of certificates awarded to any breed is based on the average registration per year over a three-year period. The following schedule for the allocation of CC's has been adopted by the English Kennel Club effective in 1975:

Three-year Registration	Total CC's
up to 200	up to 8
201-300	11
301-500	13
501-800	16
801-1,000	18
1,001-1,500	20
1,501-1,800	22
1,801-2,500	24

Provisions are made for registrations of up to 50,000, for which forty-four CC's are awarded. Such large numbers are unlikely ever to be of significance to Welsh Corgi breeders, for average registrations number in the hundreds for the Cardigan and in the low thousands for the Pembroke.

The English Kennel Club divides the entries for both dogs and bitches into eight classes: Special Puppy, for dogs six to nine months; Puppy, six to twelve months: Junior, six to eighteen months; Maiden, for dogs that have never won a first prize; Novice, for dogs that have not won a Challenge Certificate nor more than three first prizes; Graduate, for dogs that have not won a Challenge Certificate nor more than four first prizes; Open, for any dog; and Veteran, for dogs seven years or older. The English Kennel Club sponsors both Open and Championship Shows, but Challenge Certificates are only available at the Championship Shows. One of the interesting differences between judging in Great Britain and in the United States is seen in the way in which the judges report on their assignments. The comments of the English judges are regularly published in the English *Dog World,* and the judge discusses the strengths and weaknesses of each dog he placed at a show. His comments are public for all to see—both owner and competitor.

Ch. Kentwood Betsan, imported by Mrs. Michael Pym. (Photo by Thomas Fall, London.)

The German Kennel Club sponsors a World Championship Show. Breed winners here can earn, in a single show, the titles of German Champion, World Champion, and the *Certificat d'Aptitude au Championat Internationale* (CACIB) award. Each dog is given one of the following five ratings: Excellent, Very Good, Good, Satisfactory, or Unsatisfactory.

France divides its one hundred thirty recognized breeds into eight groups. The Germans divide their sixty-six breeds into five groups. Spain lists fifteen breeds in four groups.

Total dog registrations in England have risen from 11,650 in 1900 to 79,207 in 1976. The increase has been steady with the exception of the war years: 1910—18,918; 1920—16,189; 1930—48,784; 1940—13,968; 1950—100,433; 1960—133,618; and 1970—180,000. The number of breeds recognized by the English Kennel Club has risen from eighty-two in 1931, just before Corgis were accepted, to one hundred forty breeds today.

The registration figures below indicate that the Cardigan ranked eighty-eighth among English breeds in 1976 and the Pembroke ranked nineteenth.

Year	Cardigan	Pembroke
1965	241	5,706
1966	197	4,625
1967	197	4,459
1968	210	4,593
1969	192	4,165
1970	228	3,897
1971	218	2,979
1972	252	3,180
1973	223	2,936
1974	245	2,621
1975	159	1,922
1976	79	1,143

During this period approximately ten Pembrokes completed their championship each year, while only four Cardigans earned their title. During 1976 thirty-two Challenge Certificates were allocated for Cardigans to be awarded at sixteen championship shows. The Pembrokes vied for seventy Challenge Certificates at thirty-five shows.

The leading show kennels in England are listed alphabetically by kennel prefix.

Braxentra Kennel of Pembrokes is owned by Mrs. V. Palmer-Cummings of Kings Lyon. Her winners are the Best-in-Show winning International Ch. Barngremlin of Braxentra, who has eleven CC's, Ch. Barney of Braxentra, and Ch. Beretta of Braxentra.

The Caswell Pembroke Kennel of Mrs. F. G. Rainbow of Warwickshire is most famous for Ch. Caswell Duskie Knight, who earned more than thirty CC's and was the top stud dog from 1966 to 1969.

The Craythorne Pembroke Kennel of Mrs. Sheldon of Kent exported Craythorne Alibaba to Holland, where he obtained his Dutch championship, and Craythorne Prideanjoy to the United States, where she earned her American title.

The Dilwel Cardigan Kennel of Mr. and Mrs. J. H. Jones of Buckinghamshire is the breeder of Ch. Dilwel Gweno-Yr-Ad, Ch. Dilwel Auntie Maggie, and International Ch. Dilwel Maggie.

The Downholme Kennel of Mrs. A. M. Hart has the Cardigan stud Ch. Downhole Johnny Boy. Pembrokes are represented by Student Prince of Downholme.

The Dronlow Kennel of Mrs. and Miss Ludlow-Glover of Devonshire finished Ch. Dronlow Dancing Lady.

Evancoyd Kennel was established in Worcester by Mrs. B. J. Thompson. Ch. Evancoyd Personality Girl has won thirty-two CC's and Ch. Evancoyd Audacious has ten.

The Gleghornie Cardigan Kennel of Mrs. P. A. Jones is located in Devonshire. Winners include Ch. Gleghornie Brigadier, Ch. Gleghornie Elkay Miri and Ch. Gleghornie Blackthorne, who won seventeen CC's. Blackthorne is the dam of American Ch. Gleghornie Cavalier, UDT.

The Grangefield Kennel of Doreen and John Page of Leeds is the owner of Ch. Deb's Delight, who has earned fourteen CC's.

The Kentwood Kennel of Mrs. A. J. and Miss S. H. Godden raises both Cardigans and Pembrokes as well as German Shepherds. Among Corgi winners are Ch. Kentwood Brenin, Ch. Kentwood Cymro, and Ch. Kentwood Dewin.

Lees Kennel of Miss P. L. Curties of Sussex was established in 1937. In addition to Cardigans and Pembrokes, Miss Curties raises Norfolk Terriers and Whippets. The foundation stock for this kennel all goes back to Ch. Rozavel Red Dragon, who appears no less than seventy-eight times in the ten-generation pedigree of the current winner, Ch. Lees Chico. Other title holders are Ch. Lees Sunslave, Ch. Lees Cracknel, Ch. Lees Hadrian, and Ch. Lees Opalsong of Ireland. Most familiar to breeders in the United States is English, American, and Canadian Ch. Lees Symphony, who was imported by Mrs. J. Donald Duncan of Kaydon Kennel. Symphony was the sire of twenty-six American champions.

Leonine Kennel of Mr. and Mrs. E. Froggatt of Cheshire breeds Pembrokes, West Highland White, and Beagles. Among the Corgi winners are Ch. Leonine Kathis, Ch. Leonine Adonis, Ch. Leonine Tansy, and the Best-in-Show winning Leonine Christopher. The kennel is represented overseas by American and Canadian Ch. Leonine Leprechaun and American Ch. Leonine Ambertan.

Lisay Kennel was owned by Mr. and Mrs. Charles Lister-Kaye. Mr. Lister-Kaye is the author of the standard English book, *The Welsh Corgi*. His winners include: Ch. Lisaye Covertcoat, Ch. Lisay Disturbance, New Zealand Ch. Lisaye Larkspur, and Ch. Lisaye Mariella, who won twelve CC's.

Mabinogi Pembroke Kennel is owned by Mrs. Hugh Griffith of Warwickshire. Her winners include: Ch. Mabinogi Maori, International Ch. Mabinogi Martini, and Ch. Mabinogi Myrddin, who is now owned by Dronlow's Kennel.

Mynthurst Barn Kennel in Surrey is owned by Mrs. Maureen Roberts. Ch. Mynthurst Carousel of Cellohop represents the kennel at home. Exports include Mynthurst Music Master to Australia, Mynthurst Chatterer to the United States, Mynthurst Water Boatman to Germany, and Mynthurst The Wistful to New Zealand.

93

Parmel Kennel of the Parkinsons of Derbyshire is represented in Cardigans by Ch. Parmel Pilot and Ch. Parmel Dandini.

Robgwen Cardigan Kennel is owned by Mrs. Gwen Roberts of Shrewsbury. Her winners are Ch. Robgwen Welsh Minstrel and Ch. Robgwen Black Beauty. Mrs. Roberts imported American Ch. Winsdown Blue Disc and showed him to his English championship.

Rozavel Kennel of Mrs. Thelma Gray was established in Surrey in 1928. Mrs. Gray has been active in Corgis since they were recognized by the English Kennel Club. She also raises Chihuahuas and Beagles. Her first great Corgi winner was Ch. Rozavel Red Dragon, who earned twelve CC's and was the leading stud between 1934 and 1939. The first Corgi ever to go Best in Show was Ch. Rozavel Rainbow, who was exported to Mrs. A. Porter of Maryland, who showed her to her American title. Other firsts for the kennel include: International Ch. Rozavel Lucky Strike, first international champion; American Ch. Rozavel Rufus, CD, first Pembroke male to win an obedience class; and Rozavel Wild Rose, the first female obedience winner. Rozavel Field Marshall was shipped to Travis P. Shackelford and Joan Maskie in the United States, where he completed his title and became a multiple Group winner.

Saffid Kennel is owned by Mrs. Betty Faithful of Hampshire. Winning Pembrokes from this kennel are Ch. Saffid Surprise Packet and Ch. Saffid Sorceress.

The Stormerbanks Kennel of Miss P. Hewan of Berkshire is very familiar to American breeders because of the great stud, Ch. Stormerbanks Tristam of Cote de Neige. Imported by Mrs. Marjorie Butcher of Cote de Neige, he completed his championship and became the Number Two sire in the history of the breed with forty champion get. Recent winners from the kennel include: Ch. Stormerbanks Vanessa, Ch. Stormerbanks Foxyface, Ch. Stormerbanks Invader, and Ch. Stormerbanks Sabreflash.

Wey Pembroke Kennel was established in Surrey in 1948 by Mr. and Mrs. Kenneth Butler. They finished their first title holder, Ch. Lisabelle of Wey, in 1952. In 1950 Sinbad of Wey became the first Corgi to attain the Tracking degree. Twenty-two Wey Corgis earned championship titles in England and another sixty earned their titles in other countries. Ch. Sealion of Wey is an all-breed Best-in-Show winner and Ch. Sealord of Wey has his international championship. Other winners are Ch. Costons Cherokee of Wey, Ch. Seamist of Wey, and English and American Ch. Rockrose of

Wey, who was imported into the United States by Mr. and Mrs. Derek G. Rayne.

Winrod Kennel is owned by Mr. and Mrs. E. J. Busby of Stonesfield. Champions from this kennel are Ch. Winrod Pollyanna, Ch. Winrod Rhapsody, and Ch. Winrod Rob Roy.

In addition to the above list of Corgi show kennels, there are other breeders who are dedicated to the betterment of the breeds. Among these are: Banhaw Kennel, Mrs. S. Watts-Russel, Northamptonshire; Coedceirios Kennel, Miss P. E. Lewis, South Wales; Cowfolds Kennel, Miss M. Murray-Wright, Hampshire; Cwellyn Kennel, Mrs. I. E. Brooks and Miss R. Powell, Essex; Elsdyle Kennel, Mrs. B. M. Morgan, Hertfordshire; Gwenlais Kennel, Mr. and Mrs. B. A. Jones, South Wales; Drumridge Kennel, Mrs. M. R. Drummand, Antrim; Masongil Kennel, Mr. and Mrs. G. W. Peacock, Yorkshire; Medloyd Kennel, Lady Lloyd, Buckinghampshire; Pengavin Kennel, Mrs. Peggy E. Franks, Kent; Ringinglow, Miss M. Thomas, Cheshire; Robrene Kennel, Mrs. I. A. Fox, Hertfordshire; Stokeplain Kennel, Mrs. W. Irlam, Northampshire; Treland Kennel, Mrs. R. M. Tresidder, Kent; Wendac Kennel, Mrs. Doreen Dodd, Birmingham; Whielden Kennel, Miss Joan Wadge, Buckinghampshire; Winsdelf Kennel, Mrs. A. Philipson, Yorkshire; and Wyford Kennel, Mr. and Mrs. Joseph Ford, Essex.

In addition to shipping dogs to the United States, British kennels have exported show dogs to many other countries where they attained their titles. Such winners include: Swedish Ch. Kydor Cointreau, South African Ch. Lees Paladin of St. Mabyn, Rhodesian Ch. Rhoswynne Dilys, and Canadian, Bermudian, and American Ch. Convista Sunsabre of Lees, the Specialty Best-in-Show winner in Canada.

Australia also has a number of kennels breeding Welsh Corgis. Special attention was drawn to the Pembroke Ch. Bowmore Mark Time, owned by Mrs. C. Jobson, when he went Best in Show at the Melbourne Royal Show in 1974 over an entry of 4,922 dogs. In addition to Mrs. Jobson's Bowmore Kennel, there are a number of other show kennels. Included in this list are the Cardigan kennels Berylian, owned by Mrs. Beryl Black, and Kurmara, owned by Mrs. J. Brennan. Among Pembroke breeders are: Dunmerry Kennel, Mr. and Mrs. N. R. Duncan; Dygae Kennel, Mrs. D. Baillie; Goldacres Kennel, Mrs. Joan Exell; Keithvale Kennel, Mr. and Mrs. P. Carman; Narawen Kennel, Mrs. S. Gavin; Pictorela Kennel, R. N. Close; and Westglen Kennel, Mr. and Mrs. A. Cook.

English Ch. Lees
Hadrian, owned by
Miss P. L. Curties
of Sussex.

Rozavel Field
Mouse, owned by
Mrs. Thelma Gray
of Surrey.

Karin of Wey,
owned by Mrs.
Kenneth Butler of
Surrey.

Manners for the Family Dog

Although each dog has personality quirks and idiosyncrasies that set him apart as an individual, dogs in general have two characteristics that can be utilized to advantage in training. The first is the dog's strong desire to please, which has been built up through centuries of association with man. The second lies in the innate quality of the dog's mentality. It has been proved conclusively that while dogs have reasoning power, their learning ability is based on a direct association of cause and effect, so that they willingly repeat acts that bring pleasant results and discontinue acts that bring unpleasant results. Hence, to take fullest advantage of a dog's abilities, the trainer must make sure the dog understands a command, and then reward him when he obeys and correct him when he does wrong.

Commands should be as short as possible and should be repeated in the same way, day after day. Saying "Heel," one day, and "Come here and heel," the next will confuse the dog. *Heel, sit, stand, stay, down,* and *come* are standard terminology, and are preferable for a dog that may later be given advanced training.

Tone of voice is important, too. For instance, a coaxing tone helps cajole a young puppy into trying something new. Once an exercise is mastered, commands given in a firm, matter-of-fact voice give the dog confidence in his own ability. Praise, expressed in an exuberant tone, will tell the dog quite clearly that he has earned his master's approval. On the other hand, a firm "No" indicates with equal clarity that he has done wrong.

Rewards for good performance may consist simply of praising lavishly and petting the dog, although many professional trainers use bits of food as rewards. Tidbits are effective only if the dog is hungry, of course. And if you smoke, you must be sure to wash your hands before each training session, for the odor of nicotine is repulsive to dogs. On the hands of a heavy smoker, the odor of nicotine may be so strong that the dog is unable to smell the tidbit.

Correction for wrong-doing should be limited to repeating "No," in a scolding tone of voice or to confining the dog to his bed. Spanking or striking the dog is taboo—particularly using sticks, which might cause injury, but the hand should never be used either. For field training as well as some obedience work, the hand is used to signal the dog. Dogs that have been punished by slapping have a tendency to cringe whenever they see a hand raised and consequently do not respond promptly when the owner's intent is not to punish but to signal.

Some trainers recommend correcting the dog by whacking him with a rolled-up newspaper. The idea is that the newspaper will not injure the dog but that the resulting noise will condition the dog to avoid repeating the act that seemingly caused the noise. Many authorities object to this type of correction, for it may result in the dog's becoming "noise-shy"—a decided disadvantage with show dogs which must maintain poise in adverse, often noisy, situations. "Noise-shyness" is also an unfortunate reaction in field dogs, since it may lead to gun-shyness.

To be effective, correction must be administered immediately, so that in the dog's mind there is a direct connection between his act and the correction. You can make voice corrections under almost any circumstances, but you must never call the dog to you and then correct him, or he will associate the correction with the fact that he has come and will become reluctant to respond. If the dog is at a distance and doing something he shouldn't, go to him and scold him while he is still involved in wrong-doing. If this is impossible, ignore the offense until he repeats it. Then correct him properly.

Especially while a dog is young, he should be watched closely and stopped before he gets into mischief. All dogs need to do a certain amount of chewing, so to prevent your puppy's chewing something you value, provide him with his own balls and toys. Never allow him to chew cast-off slippers and then expect him to differentiate between cast-off items and those you value. Nylon stockings, wooden articles, and various other items may cause intestinal obstructions if the dog chews and swallows them, and death may result. Rubber and plastic toys may also be harmful if they are of types the dog can bite through or chew into pieces and then swallow. So it is essential that the dog be permitted to chew only on bones or toys he cannot chew up and swallow.

Serious training for obedience should not be started until a dog is a year old. But basic training in house manners should begin the day the puppy enters his new home. A puppy should never be given the run of the house but should be confined to a box or small pen except for play periods when you can devote full attention to him. The first thing to teach the dog is his name, so that whenever he hears it, he will immediately come to attention. Whenever you are near his box, talk to him, using his name repeatedly. During play periods, talk to him, pet him, and handle him, for he must be conditioned so he will not object to being handled by a veterinarian, show judge, or family friend. As the dog investigates his surroundings, watch him carefully and if he tries something he shouldn't, reprimand him with a scolding "No!" If he repeats the offense, scold him and confine him to his box, then praise him. Discipline must be prompt, consistent, and always followed with praise. Never tease the dog, and never allow others to do so. Kindness and understanding are essential to a pleasant, mutually rewarding relationship.

When the puppy is two to three months old, secure a flat, narrow leather collar and have him start wearing it (never use a harness, which will encourage tugging and pulling). After a week or so, attach a light leather lead to the collar during play sessions and let the puppy walk around, dragging the lead behind him. Then start holding the end of the lead and coaxing the puppy to come to you. He will then be fully accustomed to collar and lead when you start taking him outside while he is being housebroken.

Housebreaking can be accomplished in a matter of approximately two weeks provided you wait until the dog is mature enough to have some control over bodily functions. This is usually at about four months. Until that time, the puppy should spend most of his day confined to his penned area, with the floor covered with several thicknesses of newspapers so that he may relieve himself when necessary without damage to floors.

Either of two methods works well in housebreaking—the choice depending upon where you live. If you live in a house with a readily accessible yard, you will probably want to train the puppy from the beginning to go outdoors. If you live in an apartment without easy access to a yard, you may decide to train him first to relieve himself on newspapers and then when he has learned control, to teach the puppy to go outdoors.

If you decide to train the puppy by taking him outdoors, arrange some means of confining him indoors where you can watch him closely—in a small penned area, or tied to a short lead (five or six feet). Dogs are naturally clean animals, reluctant to soil their quarters, and confining the puppy to a limited area will encourage him to avoid making a mess.

A young puppy must be taken out often, so watch your puppy closely and if he indicates he is about to relieve himself, take him out at once. If he has an accident, scold him and take him out so he will associate the act of going outside with the need to relieve himself. Always take the puppy out within an hour after meals—preferably to the same place each time—and make sure he relieves himself before you return him to the house. Restrict his water for two hours before bedtime and take him out just before you retire for the night. When you wake in the morning, take him out again.

For paper training, set aside a particular room and cover a large area of the floor with several thicknesses of newspapers. Confine the dog on a short leash and each time he relieves himself, remove the soiled papers and replace them with clean ones.

As his control increases, gradually decrease the paper area, leaving part of the floor bare. If he uses the bare floor, scold him mildly and put him on the papers, letting him know that there is where he is to relieve himself. As he comes to understand the idea, increase the bare area until papers cover only space equal to approximately two full newspaper sheets. Keep him using the papers, but begin taking him out on a leash at the times of day that he habitually relieves himself. Watch him closely when he is indoors and at the first sign that he needs to go, take him outdoors. With this method too, restrict the puppy's water for two hours before bedtime, but if necessary, permit him to use the papers before you retire for the night.

Using either method, the puppy will be housebroken in an amazingly short time. Once he has learned control he will need to relieve himself only four or five times a day.

Informal obedience training, started at the age of about six to eight months, will provide a good background for any advanced training you may decide to give your dog later. The collar most effective for training is the metal chain-link variety. The correct size for your dog will be about one inch longer than the measurement around the largest part of his head. The chain must be slipped through one of the rings so the collar forms a loop. The collar should be put on with the loose ring at the right of the dog's neck, the chain attached to it coming over the neck and through the holding ring, rather than under the neck. Since the dog is to be at your left for most of the training, this makes the collar most effective.

The leash should be attached to the loose ring, and should be either webbing or leather, six feet long and a half inch to a full inch

Chain-link collar. The collar should be removed whenever the dog is not under your immediate supervision, for many dogs have met death by strangulation when a collar was left on and became entangled in some object.

wide. When you want your dog's attention, or wish to correct him, give a light, quick pull on the leash, which will momentarily tighten the collar about the neck. Release the pressure instantly, and the correction will have been made. If the puppy is already accustomed to a leather collar, he will adjust easily to the training collar. But before you start training sessions, practice walking with the dog until he responds readily when you increase tension on the leash.

Set aside a period of fifteen minutes, once or twice a day, for regular training sessions, and train in a place where there will be no distractions. Teach only one exercise at a time, making sure the dog has mastered it before going on to another. It will probably take at least a week for the dog to master each exercise. As training progresses, start each session by reviewing exercises the dog has already learned, then go on to the new exercise for a period of concerted practice. When discipline is required, make the correction immediately, and always praise the dog after corrections as well as when he obeys promptly. During each session stick strictly to business. Afterwards, take time to play with the dog.

The first exercise to teach is heeling. Have the dog at your left and hold the leash as shown in the illustration on the preceding page. Start walking, and just as you put your foot forward for the first step, say your dog's name to get his attention, followed by the command, "Heel!" Simultaneously, pull on the leash lightly. As you walk, try to keep the dog at your left side, with his head alongside your left leg. Pull on the leash as necessary to urge him forward or back, to right or left, but keep him in position. Each time you pull on the leash, say "Heel!" and praise the dog lavishly. When the dog heels properly in a straight line, start making circles, turning corners, etc.

Once the dog has learned to heel well, start teaching the "sit." Each time you stop while heeling, command "Sit!" The dog will be at your left, so use your left hand to press on his rear and guide him to a sitting position, while you use the leash in your right hand to keep his head up. Hold him in position for a few moments while you praise him, then give the command to heel. Walk a few steps, stop, and repeat the procedure. Before long he will automatically sit whenever you stop. You can then teach the dog to "sit" from any position.

When the dog will sit on command without correction, he is ready to learn to stay until you release him. Simply sit him, command "Stay!" and hold him in position for perhaps half a minute, repeating "Stay," if he attempts to stand. You can release him by saying "O.K." Gradually increase the time until he will stay on command for three or four minutes.

The "stand-stay" should also be taught when the dog is on leash. While you are heeling, stop and give the command "Stand!" Keep the dog from sitting by quickly placing your left arm under him, immediately in front of his right hind leg. If he continues to try to sit, don't scold him but start up again with the heel command, walk a few steps, and stop again, repeating the stand command and preventing the dog from sitting. Once the dog has mastered the stand, teach him to stay by holding him in position and repeating the word "Stay!"

The "down stay" will prove beneficial in many situations, but especially if you wish to take your dog in the car without confining him to a crate. To teach the "down," have the dog sitting at your side with collar and leash on. If he is a large dog, step forward with the leash in your hand and turn so you face him. Let the leash touch the floor, then step over it with your right foot so it is under the instep of your shoe. Grasping the leash low down with both hands, slowly pull up, saying, "Down!" Hold the leash taut until the dog goes down. Once he responds well, teach the dog to stay in the down position (the down-stay), using the same method as for the sit- and stand-stays.

To teach small dogs the "down," another method may be used. Have the dog sit at your side, then kneel beside him. Reach across his back with your left arm, and take hold of his left front leg close to the body. At the same time, with your right hand take hold of his right front leg close to his body. As you command "Down!" gently lift the legs and place the dog in the down position. Release your hold on his legs and slide your left hand onto his back, repeating, "Down, stay," while keeping him in position.

The "come" is taught when the dog is on leash and heeling. Simply walk along, then suddenly take a step backward, saying "Come!" Pull the leash as you give the command and the dog will turn and follow you. Continue walking backward, repeatedly saying "Come," and tightening the leash if necessary.

Once the dog has mastered the exercises while on leash, try taking the leash off and going through the same routine, beginning with the heeling exercise. If the dog doesn't respond promptly, he needs review with the leash on. But patience and persistence will be rewarded, for you will have a dog you can trust to respond promptly under all conditions.

Even after they are well trained, dogs sometimes develop bad habits that are hard to break. Jumping on people is a common habit, and all members of the family must assist if it is to be broken. If the dog is a large or medium breed, take a step forward and raise your knee just as he starts to jump on you. As your knee strikes the dog's chest, command "Down!" in a scolding voice. When a small dog jumps on you, take both front paws in your hands, and, while talking in a pleasant tone of voice, step on the dog's back feet just hard enough to hurt them slightly. With either method the dog is taken by surprise and doesn't associate the discomfort with the person causing it.

Occasionally a dog may be too chummy with guests who don't care for dogs. If the dog has had obedience training, simply command "Come!" When he responds, have him sit beside you.

Excessive barking is likely to bring complaints from neighbors, and persistent efforts may be needed to subdue a dog that barks without provocation. To correct the habit, you must be close to the dog when he starts barking. Encircle his muzzle with both hands, hold his mouth shut, and command "Quiet!" in a firm voice. He should soon learn to respond so you can control him simply by giving the command.

Sniffing other dogs is an annoying habit. If the dog is off leash and sniffs other dogs, ignoring your commands to come, he needs

Benching area at Westminster Kennel Club Show.

to review the lessons on basic behavior. When the dog is on leash, scold him, then pull on the leash, command "Heel," and walk away from the other dog.

A well-trained dog will be no problem if you decide to take him with you when you travel. No matter how well he responds, however, he should never be permitted off leash when you walk him in a strange area. Distractions will be more tempting, and there will be more chance of his being attacked by other dogs. So whenever the dog travels with you, take his leash along—and use it.

Judging for Best in Show at Westminster Kennel Club Show.

Show Competition

Centuries ago, it was common practice to hold agricultural fairs in conjunction with spring and fall religious festivals, and to these gatherings, cattle, dogs, and other livestock were brought for exchange. As time went on, it became customary to provide entertainment, too. Dogs often participated in such sporting events as bull baiting, bear baiting, and ratting. Then the dog that exhibited the greatest skill in the arena was also the one that brought the highest price when time came for barter or sale. Today, these fairs seem a far cry from our highly organized bench shows and field trials. But they were the forerunners of modern dog shows and played an important role in shaping the development of purebred dogs.

The first organized dog show was held at Newcastle, England, in 1859. Later that same year, a show was held at Birmingham. At both shows dogs were divided into four classes and only Pointers and Setters were entered. In 1860, the first dog show in Germany was held at Apoldo, where nearly one hundred dogs were exhibited and entries were divided into six groups. Interest expanded rapidly, and by the time the Paris Exhibition was held in 1878, the dog show was a fixture of international importance.

In the United States, the first organized bench show was held in 1874 in conjunction with the meeting of the Illinois State Sportsmen's Association in Chicago, and all entries were dogs of sporting breeds. Although the show was a rather casual affair, interest spread quickly. Before the end of the year, shows were held in Oswego, New York, Mineola, Long Island, and Memphis, Tennessee. And the latter combined a bench show with the first organized field trial ever held in the United States. In January 1875, an all-breed show (the first in the United States) was held at Detroit, Michigan. From then on, interest increased rapidly, though rules were not always uniform, for there was no organization through which to coordinate activities until September 1884 when The American Kennel Club was founded. Now the largest dog registering organization in the world, the AKC is an association of several hundred member clubs—all breed, specialty, field trial, and obedience groups—each represented by a delegate to the AKC.

The several thousand shows and trials held annually in the United States do much to stimulate interest in breeding to produce better looking, sounder, purebred dogs. For breeders, shows provide a means of measuring the merits of their work as compared with accomplishments of other breeders. For hundreds of thousands of dog fanciers, they provide an absorbing hobby.

Bench Shows

At bench (or conformation) shows, dogs are rated comparatively on their physical qualities (or conformation) in accordance with breed Standards which have been approved by The American Kennel Club. Characteristics such as size, coat, color, placement of eye or ear, general soundness, etc., are the basis for selecting the best dog in a class. Only purebred dogs are eligible to compete and if the show is one where points toward a championship are to be awarded, a dog must be at least six months old.

Bench shows are of various types. An all-breed show has classes for all of the breeds recognized by The American Kennel Club as well as a Miscellaneous Class for breeds not recognized, such as the Australian Cattle Dog, the Ibizan Hound, the Spinoni Italiani, etc. A sanctioned match is an informal meeting where dogs compete but not for championship points. A specialty show is confined to a single breed. Other shows may restrict entries to champions of record, to American-bred dogs, etc. Competition for Junior Showmanship or for Best Brace, Best Team, or Best Local Dog may be included. Also, obedience competition is held in conjunction with many bench shows.

The term "bench show" is somewhat confusing in that shows of this type may be either "benched" or "unbenched." At the former, each dog is assigned an individual numbered stall where he must remain throughout the show except for times when he is being judged, groomed, or exercised. At unbenched shows, no stalls are provided and dogs are kept in their owners' cars or in crates when not being judged.

A show where a dog is judged for conformation actually constitutes an elimination contest. To begin with, the dogs of a single breed compete with others of their breed in one of the regular classes: Puppy, Novice, Bred by Exhibitor, American-Bred, or

Open, and, finally, Winners, where the top dogs of the preceding five classes meet. The next step is the judging for Best of Breed (or Best of Variety of Breed). Here the Winners Dog and Winners Bitch (or the dog named Winners if only one prize is awarded) compete with any champions that are entered, together with any undefeated dogs that have competed in additional non-regular classes. The dog named Best of Breed (or Best of Variety of Breed), then goes on to compete with the other Best of Breed winners in his Group. The dogs that win in Group competition then compete for the final and highest honor, Best in Show.

When the Winners Class is divided by sex, championship points are awarded the Winners Dog and Winners Bitch. If the Winners Class is not divided by sex, championship points are awarded the dog or bitch named Winners. The number of points awarded varies, depending upon such factors as the number of dogs competing, the Schedule of Points established by the Board of Directors of the AKC, and whether the dog goes on to win Best of Breed, the Group, and Best in Show.

In order to become a champion, a dog must win fifteen points, including points from at least two major wins—that is, at least two shows where three or more points are awarded. The major wins must be under two different judges, and one or more of the remaining points must be won under a third judge. The most points ever awarded at a show is five and the least is one, so, in order to become a champion, a dog must be exhibited and win in at least three shows, and usually he is shown many times before he wins his championship.

Pure Bred Dogs—American Kennel Gazette and other dog magazines contain lists of forthcoming shows, together with names and addresses of sponsoring organizations to which you may write for entry forms and information relative to fees, closing dates, etc. Before entering your dog in a show for the first time, you should familiarize yourself with the regulations and rules governing competition. You may secure such information from The American Kennel Club or from a local dog club specializing in your breed. It is essential that you also familiarize yourself with the AKC approved Standard for your breed so you will be fully aware of characteristics worthy of merit as well as those considered faulty, or possibly even serious enough to disqualify the dog from competition. For instance, monorchidism (failure of one testicle to descend) and cryptorchidism (failure of both testicles to descend) are disqualifying faults in all breeds.

If possible, you should first attend a show as a spectator and observe judging procedures from ringside. It will also be helpful to join a local breed club and to participate in sanctioned matches before entering an all-breed show.

The dog should be equipped with a narrow leather show lead and a show collar—never an ornamented or spiked collar. For benched shows, either a bench crate or a metal-link bench chain to fasten the dog to the bench will be needed. For unbenched shows, the dog's crate should be taken along so that he may be confined in comfort when he is not appearing in the ring. A dog should never be left in a car with all the windows closed. In hot weather the temperature will become unbearable in a very short time. Heat exhaustion may result from even a short period of confinement, and death may ensue.

Food and water dishes will be needed, as well as a supply of the food and water to which the dog is accustomed. Brushes and combs are also necessary, so that you may give the dog's coat a final grooming after you arrive at the show.

Familiarize yourself with the schedule of classes ahead of time, for the dog must be fed and exercised and permitted to relieve himself, and any last-minute grooming completed before his class is called. Both you and the dog should be ready to enter the ring unhurriedly. A good deal of skill in conditioning, training, and handling is required if a dog is to be presented properly. And it is essential that the handler himself be composed, for a jittery handler will transmit his nervousness to his dog.

Once the class is assembled in the ring, the judge will ask that the dogs be paraded in line, moving counter-clockwise in a circle. If you have trained your dog well, you will have no difficulty controlling him in the ring, where he must change pace quickly and gracefully and walk and trot elegantly and proudly with head erect. The show dog must also stand quietly for inspection, posing like a statue for several minutes while the judge observes his structure in detail, examines teeth, feet, coat, etc. When the judge calls your dog forward for individual inspection, do not attempt to converse, but answer any questions he may ask.

As the judge examines the class, he measures each dog against the ideal described in the Standard, then measures the dogs against each other in a comparative sense and selects for first place the dog that comes closest to conforming to the Standard for its breed. If your dog isn't among the winners, don't grumble. If he places first, don't brag loudly. For a bad loser is disgusting, but a poor winner is insufferable.

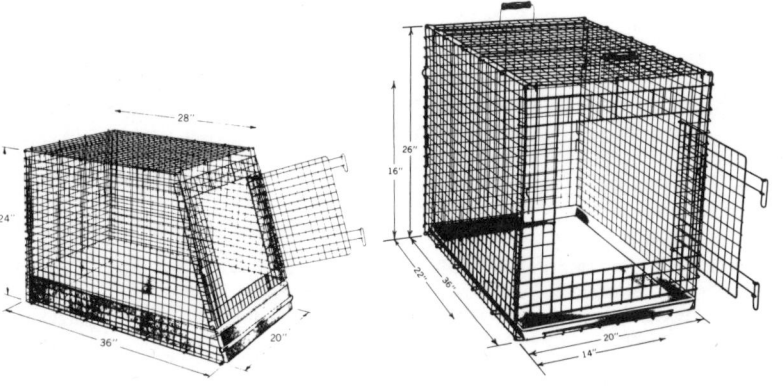

Junior Showmanship Competition at Westminster Kennel Club Show.

Bench crate.

Wagon crate.

Collars. At the top are two "pinch" or "spiked" collars that are not permitted in AKC shows. Below are two permissible "choke" collars, the one on the right of steel chain and the one on the left of braided nylon. While the choke collars are permitted in conformation shows, they are used more often in obedience competition.

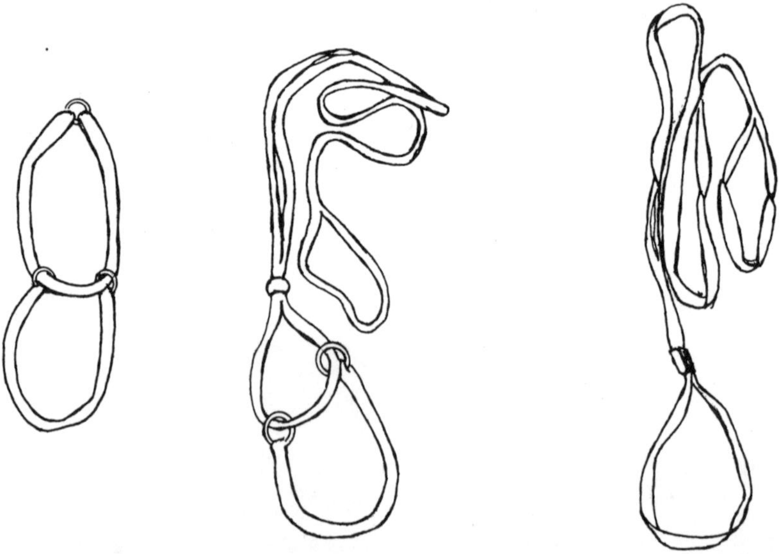

Left, "English" or "Martingale" collar to which lead would be attached. Center, "English" or "Martingale" collar and lead. In using either of these, the dog's head would be inserted through the lower loop. Right, nylon slip lead. Collars and leads of these three types are preferred for conformation showing because they give better control for stacking a dog than the "choke" collars.

Obedience Competition

For hundreds of years, dogs have been used in England and Germany in connection with police and guard work, and their working potential has been evaluated through tests devised to show agility, strength, and courage. Organized training has also been popular with English and German breeders for many years, although it was first practiced primarily for the purpose of training large breeds in aggressive tactics.

There was little interest in obedience training in the United States until 1933 when Mrs. Whitehouse Walker returned from England and enthusiastically introduced the sport. Two years later, Mrs. Walker persuaded The American Kennel Club to approve organized obedience activities and to assume jurisdiction over obedience rules. Since then, interest has increased at a phenomenal rate, for obedience competition is not only a sport the average spectator can follow readily, but also a sport for which the average owner can train his own dog easily. Obedience competition is suitable for all breeds. Furthermore, there is no limit to the number of dogs that may win in competition, for each dog is scored individually on the basis of a point rating system.

The dog is judged on his response to certain commands, and if he gains a high enough score in three successive trials under different judges, he wins an obedience degree. Degrees awarded are "CD"—Companion Dog; "CDX"—Companion Dog Excellent; and "UD"—Utility Dog. A fourth degree, the "TD" or Tracking Dog degree, may be won at any time and tests for it are held apart from dog shows. The qualifying score is a minimum of 170 points out of a possible total of 200, with no score in any one exercise less than 50% of the points allotted.

Since obedience titles are progressive, earlier titles (with the exception of the tracking degree) are dropped as a dog acquires the next higher degree. If an obedience title is gained in another country in addition to the United States, that fact is signified by the word "International," followed by the title.

Trials for obedience trained dogs are held at most of the larger bench shows, and obedience training clubs are to be found in almost all communities today. Information concerning forthcoming trials and lists of obedience training clubs are included regularly in *Pure Bred Dogs–American Kennel Gazette*—and other dog magazines. Pamphlets containing rules and regulations governing obedience competition are available upon request from The American Kennel Club, 51 Madison Avenue, New York, N.Y. 10010. Rules are revised occasionally, so if you are interested in participating in obedience competition, you should be sure your copy of the regulations is current.

All dogs must comply with the same rules, although in broad jump, high jump, and bar jump competition, the jumps are adjusted to the size of the breed. Classes at obedience trials are divided into Novice (A and B), Open (A and B), and Utility (which may be divided into A and B, at the option of the sponsoring club and with the approval of The American Kennel Club).

The Novice class is for dogs that have not won the title Companion Dog. In Novice A, no person who has previously handled a dog that has won a CD title in the obedience ring at a licensed or member trial, and no person who has regularly trained such a dog, may enter or handle a dog. The handler must be the dog's owner or a member of the owner's immediate family. In Novice B, dogs may be handled by the owner or any other person.

The Open A class is for dogs that have won the CD title but have not won the CDX title. Obedience judges and licensed handlers may not enter or handle dogs in this class. Each dog must be handled by the owner or by a member of his immediate family. The Open B class is for dogs that have won the title CD or CDX. A dog may continue to compete in this class after it has won the title UD. Dogs in this class may be handled by the owner or any other person.

The Utility class is for dogs that have won the title CDX. Dogs that have won the title UD may continue to compete in this class, and dogs may be handled by the owner or any other person. Provided the AKC approves, a club may choose to divide the Utility class into Utility A and Utility B. When this is done, the Utility A class is for dogs that have won the title CDX and have not won the title UD. Obedience judges and licensed handlers may not enter or handle dogs in this class. All other dogs that are eligible for the Utility class but not eligible for Utility A may be entered in Utility B.

Novice competition includes such exercises as heeling on and off lead, the stand for examination, coming on recall, and the long sit and the long down.

In Open competition, the dog must perform such exercises as heeling free, the drop on recall, and the retrieve on the flat and over the high jump. Also, he must execute the broad jump, and the long sit and long down.

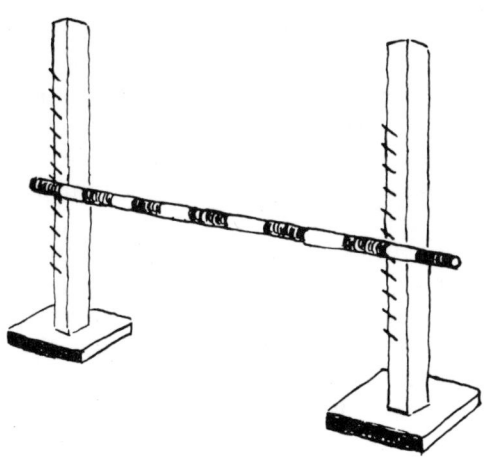

Bar Jump.

In the Utility class, competition includes scent discrimination, the directed retrieve, the signal exercise, directed jumping, and the group examination.

Tracking is the most difficult test. It is always done out-of-doors, of course, and, for obvious reasons, cannot be held at a dog show. The dog must follow a scent trail that is about a quarter mile in length. He is also required to find a scent object (glove, wallet, or other article) left by a stranger who has walked the course to lay down the scent. The dog is required to follow the trail a half to two hours after the scent is laid.

An ideal way to train a dog for obedience competition is to join an obedience class or a training club. In organized class work, beginners' classes cover pretty much the same exercises as those described in the chapter on manners. However, through class work you will develop greater precision than is possible in training your dog by yourself. Amateur handlers often cause the dog to be penalized, for if the handler fails to abide by the rules, it is the dog that suffers the penalty. A common infraction of the rules is using more than one signal or command where regulations stipulate only one may be used. Classwork will help eliminate such errors, which the owner may make unconsciously if he is working alone. Working with a class will also acquaint both dog and handler with ring procedure so that obedience trials will not present unforeseen problems.

Thirty or forty owners and dogs often comprise a class, and exercises are performed in unison, with individual instruction provided if it is required. The procedure followed in training—in fact, even wording of various commands—may vary from instructor to instructor. Equipment used will vary somewhat, also, but will usually include a training collar and leash, a long line, a dumbbell, and a jumping stick. The latter may be a short length of heavy doweling or a broom handle and both it and the dumbbell are usually painted white for increased visibility.

A bitch in season must never be taken to a training class, so before enrolling a female dog, you should determine whether she may be expected to come into season before classes are scheduled to end. If you think she will, it is better to wait and enroll her in a later course, rather than start the course and then miss classes for several weeks.

In addition to the time devoted to actual work in class, the dog must have regular, daily training sessions for practice at home. Before each class or home training session, the dog should be exercised so he will not be highly excited when the session starts, and he must be given an opportunity to relieve himself before the session begins. (Should he have an accident during the class, it is your responsibility to clean up after him.) The dog should be fed several hours before time for the class to begin or else after the class is over—never just before going to class.

If you decide to enter your dog in obedience competition, it is well to enter a small, informal show the first time. Dogs are usually called in the order in which their names appear in the catalog, so as soon as you arrive at the show, acquaint yourself with the schedule. If your dog is not the first to be judged, spend some time at ringside, observing the routine so you will know what to expect when your dog's turn comes.

In addition to collar, leash, and other equipment, you should take your dog's food and water pans and a supply of the food and water to which he is accustomed. You should also take his brushes and combs in order to give him a last-minute brushing before you enter the ring. It is important that the dog look his best even though he isn't to be judged on his appearance.

Before entering the ring, exercise your dog, give him a drink of water, and permit him to relieve himself. Once your dog enters the ring, give him your full attention and be sure to give voice commands distinctly so he will hear and understand, for there will be many distractions at ringside.

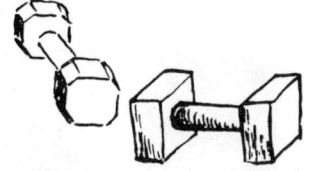

Dumbbells.

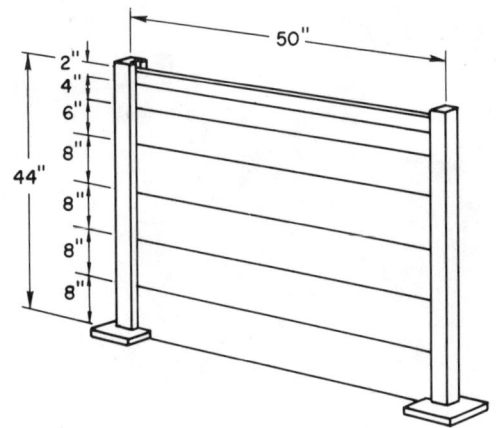

Solid hurdle.

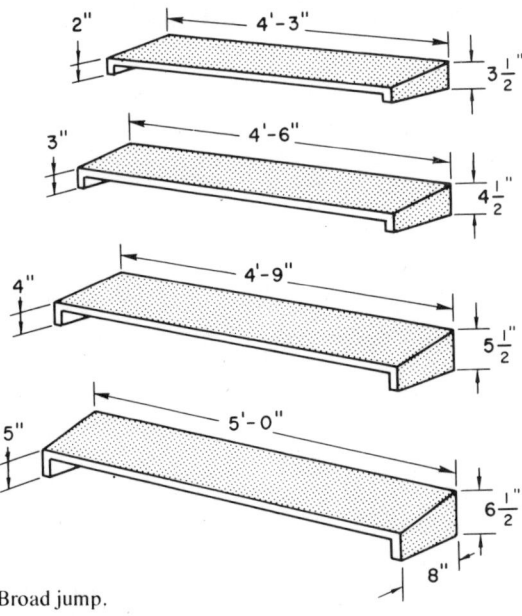

Broad jump.

Top dogs in Utility Class. This illustrates the variety of breeds that compete in obedience.

Genetics

Genetics, the science of heredity, deals with the processes by which physical and mental traits of parents are transmitted to offspring. For centuries, man has been trying to solve these puzzles, but only in the last two hundred years has significant progress been made.

During the eighteenth century, Kölreuter, a German scientist, made revolutionary discoveries concerning plant sexuality and hybridization but was unable to explain just how hereditary processes worked. In the middle of the nineteenth century, Gregor Johann Mendel, an Augustinian monk, experimented with the ordinary garden pea and made other discoveries of major significance. He found that an inherited characteristic was inherited as a complete unit, and that certain characteristics predominated over others. Next, he observed that the hereditary characteristics of each parent are contained in each offspring, even when they are not visible, and that "hidden" characteristics can be transferred without change in their nature to the grandchildren, or even later generations. Finally, he concluded that although heredity contains an element of uncertainty, some things are predictable on the basis of well-defined mathematical laws.

Unfortunately, Mendel's published paper went unheeded, and when he died in 1884 he was still virtually unknown to the scientific world. But other researchers were making discoveries, too. In 1900, three different scientists reported to learned societies that much of their research in hereditary principles had been proved years before by Gregor Mendel and that findings matched perfectly.

Thus, hereditary traits were proved to be transmitted through the chromosomes found in pairs in every living being, one of each pair contributed by the mother, the other by the father. Within each chromosome have been found hundreds of smaller structures, or genes, which are the actual determinants of hereditary characteristics. Some genes are dominant and will be seen in the offspring. Others are recessive and will not be outwardly apparent, yet can be passed on to the offspring to combine with a similar recessive gene of the other parent and thus be seen. Or they may be passed on to the offspring, not be outwardly apparent, but be passed on again to become apparent in a later generation.

Once the genetic theory of inheritance became widely known, scientists began drawing a well-defined line between inheritance and environment. More recent studies show some overlapping of these influences and indicate a combination of the two may be responsible for certain characteristics. For instance, studies have proved that extreme cold increases the amount of black pigment in the skin and hair of the "Himalayan" rabbit, although it has little or no effect on the white or colored rabbit. Current research also indicates that even though characteristics are determined by the genes, some environmental stress occurring at a particular period of pregnancy might cause physical change in the embryo.

Long before breeders had any knowledge of genetics, they practiced one of its most important principles—selective breeding. Experience quickly showed that "like begets like," and by breeding like with like and discarding unlike offspring, the various individual breeds were developed to the point where variations were relatively few. Selective breeding is based on the idea of maintaining the quality of a breed at the highest possible level, while improving whatever defects are prevalent. It requires that only the top dogs in a litter be kept for later breeding, and that inferior specimens be ruthlessly eliminated.

In planning any breeding program, the first requisite is a definite goal—that is, to have clearly in mind a definite picture of the type of dog you wish eventually to produce. To attempt to breed perfection is to approach the problem unrealistically. But if you don't breed for improvement, it is preferable that you not breed at all.

As a first step, you should select a bitch that exemplifies as many of the desired characteristics as possible and mate her with a dog that also has as many of the desired characteristics as possible. If you start with mediocre pets, you will produce mediocre pet puppies. If you decide to start with more than one bitch, all should closely approach the type you desire, since you will then stand a better chance of producing uniformly good puppies from all. Breeders often start with a single bitch and keep the best bitches in every succeeding generation.

Experienced breeders look for "prepotency" in breeding stock—that is, the ability of a dog or bitch to transmit traits to most or all of its offspring. While the term is usually used to describe the transmission of good qualities, a dog may also be prepotent in

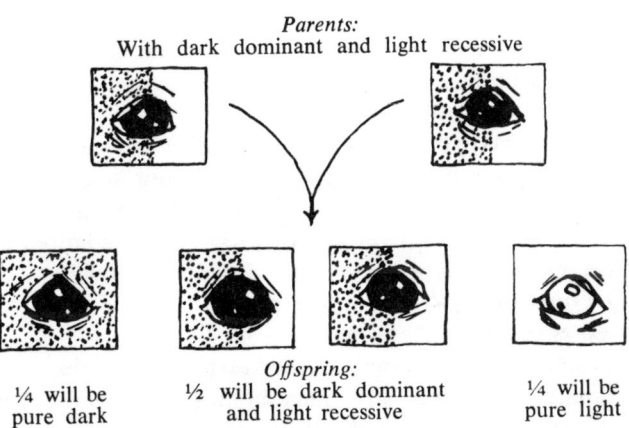

Parents:
One pure dark eyes
and one pure light eyes

Dark eyes   Light eyes

Offspring:
Eyes dark (dominant) with light recessive

Parents:
With dark dominant and light recessive

¼ will be   *Offspring:*   ¼ will be
pure dark   ½ will be dark dominant   pure light
                 and light recessive

The above is a schematic representation of the Mendelian law as it applies to the inheritance of eye color. The law applies in the same way to the inheritance of other physical characteristics.

transmitting faults. To be prepotent in a practical sense, a dog must possess many characteristics controlled by dominant genes. If desired characteristics are recessive, they will be apparent in the offspring only if carried by both sire and dam. Prepotent dogs and bitches usually come from a line of prepotent ancestors, but the mere fact that a dog has exceptional ancestors will not necessarily mean that he himself will produce exceptional offspring.

A single dog may sire a tremendous number of puppies, whereas a bitch can produce only a comparatively few litters during her lifetime. Thus, a sire's influence may be very widespread as compared to that of a bitch. But in evaluating a particular litter, it must be remembered that the bitch has had as much influence as has had the dog.

Inbreeding, line-breeding, outcrossing, or a combination of the three are the methods commonly used in selective breeding.

Inbreeding is the mating together of closely related animals, such as father-daughter, mother-son, or brother-sister. Although some breeders insist such breeding will lead to the production of defective individuals, it is through rigid inbreeding that all breeds of dogs have been established. Controlled tests have shown that any harmful effects appear within the first five or ten generations, and that if rigid selection is exercised from the beginning, a vigorous inbred strain will be built up.

Line-breeding is also the mating together of individuals related by family lines. However, matings are made not so much on the basis of the dog's and bitch's relationship to each other, but, instead, on the basis of their relationship to a highly admired ancestor, with a view to perpetuating that ancestor's qualities. Line-breeding constitutes a long-range program and cannot be accomplished in a single generation.

Outcrossing is the breeding together of two dogs that are unrelated in family lines. Actually, since breeds have been developed through the mating of close relatives, all dogs within any given breed are related to some extent. There are few breedings that are true outcrosses, but if there is no common ancestor within five generations, a mating is usually considered an outcross.

Experienced breeders sometimes outcross for one generation in order to eliminate a particular fault, then go back to inbreeding or line-breeding. Neither the good effects nor the bad effects of outcrossing can be truly evaluated in a single mating, for undesirable recessive traits may be introduced into a strain, yet not show up for several generations. Outcrossing is better left to experienced breeders, for continual outcrossing results in a wide variation in type and great uncertainty as to the results that may be expected.

Two serious defects that are believed heritable—subluxation and orchidism—should be zealously guarded against, and afflicted dogs and their offspring should be eliminated from breeding programs. Subluxation is a condition of the hip joint where the bone of the socket is eroded and the head of the thigh bone is also worn away, causing lameness which becomes progressively more serious until the dog is unable to walk. Orchidism is the failure of one or both testicles to develop and descend properly. When one testicle is involved, the term "monorchid" is used. When both are involved, "cryptorchid" is used. A cryptorchid is almost always sterile, whereas a monorchid is usually fertile. There is evidence that orchidism "runs in families" and that a monorchid transmits the tendency through bitch and male puppies alike.

Through the years, many misconceptions concerning heredity have been perpetuated. Perhaps the one most widely perpetuated is the idea evolved hundreds of years ago that somehow characteristics were passed on through the mixing of the blood of the parents. We still use terminology evolved from that theory when we speak of bloodlines, or describe individuals as full-blooded, despite the fact that the theory was disproved more than a century ago.

Also inaccurate and misleading is any statement that a definite fraction or proportion of an animal's inherited characteristics can be positively attributed to a particular ancestor. Individuals lacking knowledge of genetics sometimes declare that an individual receives half his inherited characteristics from each parent, a quarter from each grandparent, an eighth from each great-grandparent, etc. Thousands of volumes of scientific findings have been published, but no simple way has been found to determine positively which characteristics have been inherited from which ancestors, for the science of heredity is infinitely complex.

Any breeder interested in starting a serious breeding program should study several of the books on canine genetics and breeding and whelping that are currently available. Two excellent works covering these subjects are *Meisen Breeding Manual*, by Hilda Meisenzahl, and *The Standard Book of Dog Breeding*, by Dr. Alvin Grossman—both published by the publisher of this book.

Whelping box. Detail at right shows proper side-wall construction which helps keep small puppies confined and provides sheltered nook to prevent crushing or smothering.

Breeding and Whelping

The breeding life of a bitch begins when she comes into season the first time at the age of eight to ten months. Thereafter, she will come in season at roughly six-month intervals. Her maximum fertility builds up from puberty to full maturity and then declines until a state of total sterility is reached in old age. Just when this occurs is hard to determine, for the fact that an older bitch shows signs of being in season doesn't necessarily mean she is still capable of reproducing.

The length of the season varies from eighteen to twenty-one days. The first indication is a pronounced swelling of the vulva with coincidental bleeding (called "showing color") for about the first seven to nine days. The discharge gradually turns to a creamy color, and it is during this phase (estrus), from about the tenth to the fifteenth days, that the bitch is ovulating and is receptive to the male. The ripe, unfertilized ova survive for about seventy-two hours. If fertilization doesn't occur, the ova die and are discharged the next time the bitch comes in season. If fertilization does take place, each ovum attaches itself to the walls of the uterus, a membrane forms to seal it off, and a foetus develops from it.

Following the estrus phase, the bitch is still in season until about the twenty-first day and will continue to be attractive to males, although she will usually fight them off as she did the first few days. Nevertheless, to avoid accidental mating, the bitch must be confined for the entire period. Virtual imprisonment is necessary, for male dogs display uncanny abilities in their efforts to reach a bitch in season.

The odor that attracts the males is present in the bitch's urine, so it is advisable to take her a good distance from the house before permitting her to relieve herself. To eliminate problems completely, your veterinarian can prescribe a preparation that will disguise the odor but will not interfere with breeding when the time is right. Many fanciers use such preparations when exhibiting a bitch and find that nearby males show no interest whatsoever. But it is not advisable to permit a bitch to run loose when she has been given a product of this type, for during estrus she will seek the company of male dogs and an accidental mating may occur.

A potential brood bitch, regardless of breed, should have good bone, ample breadth and depth of ribbing, and adequate room in the pelvic region. Unless a bitch is physically mature—well beyond the puppy stage when she has her first season—breeding should be delayed until her second or a later season. Furthermore, even though it is possible for a bitch to conceive twice a year, she should not be bred oftener than once a year. A bitch that is bred too often will age prematurely and her puppies are likely to lack vigor.

Two or three months before a bitch is to be mated, her physical condition should be considered carefully. If she is too thin, provide a rich, balanced diet plus the regular exercise needed to develop strong, supple muscles. Daily exercise on the lead is as necessary for the too-thin bitch as for the too-fat one, although the latter will need more exercise and at a brisker pace, as well as a reduction of food, if she is to be brought to optimum condition. A prospective brood bitch must have had permanent distemper shots as well as rabies vaccination. And a month before her season is due, a veterinarian should examine a stool specimen for worms. If there is evidence of infestation, the bitch should be wormed.

A dog may be used at stud from the time he reaches physical maturity, well on into old age. The first time your bitch is bred, it is well to use a stud that has already proven his ability by having sired other litters. The fact that a neighbor's dog is readily available should not influence your choice, for to produce the best puppies, you must select the stud most suitable from a genetic standpoint.

If the stud you prefer is not going to be available at the time your bitch is to be in season, you may wish to consult your veterinarian concerning medications available for inhibiting the onset of the season. With such preparations, the bitch's season can be delayed indefinitely.

Usually the first service will be successful. However, if it isn't, in most cases an additional service is given free, provided the stud dog is still in the possession of the same owner. If the bitch misses, it may be because her cycle varies widely from normal. Through microscopic examination, a veterinarian can determine exactly when the bitch is entering the estrus phase and thus is likely to conceive.

The owner of the stud should give you a stud-service certificate, providing a four-generation pedigree for the sire and showing the date of mating. The litter registration application is completed only after the puppies are whelped, but it, too, must be signed by the owner of the stud as well as the owner of the bitch. Registration forms may be secured by writing The American Kennel Club.

In normal pregnancy there is visible enlargement of the abdomen by the end of the fifth week. By palpation (feeling with the fingers) a veterinarian may be able to distinguish developing puppies as early as three weeks after mating, but it is unwise for a novice to poke and prod, and try to detect the presence of unborn puppies.

The gestation period normally lasts nine weeks, although it may vary from sixty-one to sixty-five days. If it goes beyond sixty-five days from the date of mating, a veterinarian should be consulted.

During the first four or five weeks, the bitch should be permitted her normal amount of activity. As she becomes heavier, she should be walked on the lead, but strenuous running and jumping should be avoided. Her diet should be well balanced (see page 41), and if she should become constipated, small amounts of mineral oil may be added to her food.

A whelping box should be secured about two weeks before the puppies are due, and the bitch should start then to use it as her bed so she will be accustomed to it by the time puppies arrive. Preferably, the box should be square, with each side long enough so that the bitch can stretch out full length and have several inches to spare at either end. The bottom should be padded with an old cotton rug or other material that is easily laundered. Edges of the padding should be tacked to the floor of the box so the puppies will not get caught in it and smother. Once it is obvious labor is about to begin, the padding should be covered with several layers of spread-out newspapers. Then, as papers become soiled, the top layer can be pulled off, leaving the area clean.

Forty-eight to seventy-two hours before the litter is to be whelped, a definite change in the shape of the abdomen will be noted. Instead of looking barrel-shaped, the abdomen will sag pendulously. Breasts usually redden and become enlarged, and milk may be present a day or two before the puppies are whelped. As the time becomes imminent, the bitch will probably scratch and root at her bedding in an effort to make a nest, and will refuse food and ask to be let out every few minutes. But the surest sign is a drop in temperature of two or three degrees about twelve hours before labor begins.

The bitch's abdomen and flanks will contract sharply when labor actually starts, and for a few minutes she will attempt to expel a puppy, then rest for a while and try again. Someone should stay with the bitch the entire time whelping is taking place, and if she appears to be having unusual difficulties, a veterinarian should be called.

Puppies are usually born head first, though some may be born feet first and no difficulty encountered. Each puppy is enclosed in a separate membranous sac that the bitch will remove with her teeth. She will sever the umbilical cord, which will be attached to the soft, spongy afterbirth that is expelled right after the puppy emerges. Usually the bitch eats the afterbirth, so it is necessary to watch and make sure one is expelled for each puppy whelped. If afterbirth is retained, the bitch may develop peritonitis and die.

The dam will lick and nuzzle each newborn puppy until it is warm and dry and ready to nurse. If puppies arrive so close together that she can't take care of them, you can help her by rubbing the puppies dry with a soft cloth. If several have been whelped but the bitch continues to be in labor, all but one should be removed and placed in a small box lined with clean towels and warmed to about seventy degrees. The bitch will be calmer if one puppy is left with her at all times.

Whelping sometimes continues as long as twenty-four hours for a very large litter, but a litter of two or three puppies may be whelped in an hour. When the bitch settles down, curls around the puppies and nuzzles them to her, it usually indicates that all have been whelped.

The bitch should be taken away for a few minutes while you clean the box and arrange clean padding. If her coat is soiled, sponge it clean before she returns to the puppies. Once she is back in the box, offer her a bowl of warm beef broth and a pan of cool water, placing both where she will not have to get up in order to reach them. As soon as she indicates interest in food, give her a generous bowl of chopped meat to which codliver oil and dicalcium phosphate have been added.

If inadequate amounts of calcium are provided during the period the puppies are nursing, eclampsia may develop. Symptoms are violent trembling, rapid rise in temperature, and rigidity of muscles. Veterinary assistance must be secured immediately, for death may result in a very short time. Treatment consists of massive doses of calcium gluconate administered intravenously, after which symptoms subside in a miraculously short time.

126

For weak or very small puppies, supplemental feeding is often recommended. Any one of three different methods may be used: tube-feeding (with a catheter attached to a syringe), using an eyedropper (this method requires great care in order to avoid getting formula in the lungs), or using a tiny bottle (the "pet nurser" available at most pet supply stores). The commercially prepared puppy formulas are most convenient and are readily obtainable from a veterinarian, who can also tell you which method of administering the formula is most practical in your particular case. It is important to remember that equipment must be kept scrupulously clean. It can be sterilized by boiling, or it may be soaked in a Clorox solution, then washed carefully and dried between feedings.

All puppies are born blind and their eyes open when they are ten to fourteen days old. At first the eyes have a bluish cast and appear weak, and the puppies must be protected from strong light until at least ten days after the eyes open.

To ensure proper emotional development, young dogs should be shielded from loud noises and rough handling. Being lifted by the front legs is painful and may result in permanent injury to the shoulders. So when lifting a puppy, always place one hand under the chest with the forefinger between the front legs, and place the other hand under his bottom.

Flannelized rubber sheeting is an ideal surface for the bottom of the bed for the new puppies. It is inexpensive and washable, and will provide a surface that will give the puppies traction so that they will not slip either while nursing or when learning to walk.

Sometimes the puppies' nails are so long and sharp that they scratch the bitch's breasts. Since the nails are soft, they can be trimmed with ordinary scissors.

At about four weeks of age, formula should be provided. The amount fed each day should be increased over a period of two weeks, when the puppies can be weaned completely. One of the commercially prepared formulas can be mixed according to directions on the container, or formula can be prepared at home in accordance with instructions from a veterinarian. The formula should be warmed to lukewarm, and poured into a shallow pan placed on the floor of the box. After his mouth has been dipped into the mixture a few times, a puppy will usually start to lap formula. All puppies should be allowed to eat from the same pan, but be sure the small ones get their share. If they are pushed aside, feed them separately. Permit the puppies to nurse part of the time, but gradually increase the number of meals of formula. By the

127

time the puppies are five weeks old, the dam should be allowed with them only at night. When they are about six weeks old, they should be weaned completely. Three meals a day are usually sufficient from this time until the puppies are about three months old, when feedings are reduced to two a day. About the time the dog reaches one year of age, feedings may be reduced to one each day. (For further information on this subject, see page 38.)

Once they are weaned, puppies should be given temporary distemper injections every two weeks until they are old enough for permanent inoculations. At six weeks, stool specimens should be checked for worms, for almost without exception, puppies become infested. Specimens should be checked again at eight weeks, and as often thereafter as your veterinarian recommends.

Sometimes owners decide as a matter of convenience to have a bitch spayed or a male castrated. While this is recommended when a dog has a serious inheritable defect or when abnormalities of reproductive organs develop, in sound, normal purebred dogs, spaying a bitch or castrating a male may prove a definite disadvantage. The operations automatically bar dogs from competing in shows as well as precluding use for breeding. The operations are seldom dangerous, but they should not be performed without serious consideration of these facts.